Chinese Mandarin
PHRASE
BOOK

Kan Qian

Consultant:
Lucia Woods

BBC Books

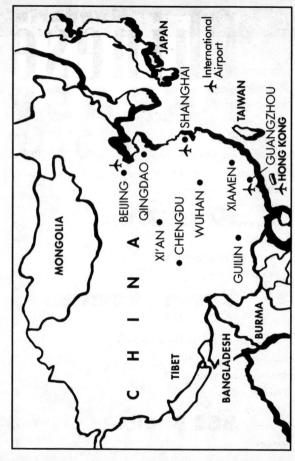

Contents

How to use this book

▌ Being able to communicate with Chinese speakers is not as difficult as many people believe. A few words plus facial expressions and gestures can convey a lot. Understanding what the locals say, even if only a little, and making yourself understood is a rewarding experience which will make your visit or stay much more interesting and enjoyable.

▌ Don't worry about getting things wrong. Please remember that you don't have to pronounce everything perfectly. The Chinese will appreciate your efforts and will try to help you. Through language, you will meet new people, make new friends, and understand the Chinese culture better.

▌ It's a good idea to prepare in advance what you want to say before the event. For example, before going shopping, check the section on shopping and the dictionary at the back so that you feel more confident.

▌ The PRONUNCIATION GUIDE provides tips on pronouncing the sounds and tones of Mandarin Chinese sounds and tones. As the tones and several sounds are completely different from those of European languages, you are strongly advised to start by studying the pronunciation guide and to return to this section as often as possible.

▌ It is also useful to have a good look at the BASIC GRAMMAR section, which provides you with the basic structures and unique features of the Chinese language so that you will have at least a rough idea of how the language works.

▌ Those who wish to understand the basics of reading and writing Chinese characters can go to the section entitled UNDERSTANDING CHINESE CHARACTERS.

▌ GENERAL PHRASES provides you with some tips and a list of basic phrases preceding the main sections.

■ The main section of the book is divided up according to different situations. Each section contains all or some of the following:

- Useful tips and information on the theme of the section
- Useful signs or other information you may see in characters
- Useful words
- Phrases you may want to say
- Things you may hear other people say to you

■ Whenever necessary or helpful, the literal translation is given in brackets, marked by *lit.*

■ The REFERENCE SECTION starts on page 131.

■ SIGNS AND NOTICES is a collection of the entries listed in the **You may see** sections throughout the book

■ The DICTIONARY is a collection of around 3000 commonly used English words with their Chinese equivalents in **pinyin** (Romanised form NOT Chinese script). You may find that many of the phrases in the main sections can be adapted simply by using another word from the DICTIONARY.

■ Enjoy your stay in China and enjoy speaking Chinese.

Pronunciation guide

▌ Some people in the West think that Cantonese is a different language from Chinese but in actual fact Cantonese is just one of the eight major dialects of the Chinese language. These dialects share the same written language but differ immensely in pronunciation. The good news is that there is a modern standard form of spoken language which is spoken (although with local accents) and understood by the majority of the population. This standard form is known as **Putonghua** (common speech) in mainland China, as **Guoyu** or **Huayu** in Taiwan, Hong Kong, and other overseas Chinese communities, and as 'Mandarin Chinese' in English-speaking countries. The term **Zhongwen** or **Hanyu** refers to the Chinese language as a whole. When Chinese people ask foreigners if they speak Chinese, they often use **Zhongwen** or **Hanyu** rather than **putonghua** as it is very unlikely that a foreigner would speak a dialect. Chinese in this book means **Putonghua**, i.e. Mandarin Chinese.

▌ **Pinyin** is the official system adopted in the People's Republic of China in 1958 to transcribe Chinese sounds into the Latin script. **Pinyin** is now adopted almost universally for transliterating Chinese personal names and place names (e.g. **Peking** was the old spelling and **Beijing** is the **pinyin** spelling). The transliteration system used in this book is **pinyin**.

▌ Most Chinese words are made up of one syllable. A syllable may consist of a single vowel, a compound vowel (e.g. ou, ei, ing) or a vowel preceded by a consonant. Sounds that appear before vowels are called 'initials' (like 'consonants' in English) and the remaining sounds are called 'finals' (i.e. vowels and vowels with a nasal sound). Each syllable is represented by a Chinese character.

▌ Compared with some other languages, Chinese has fewer sounds – 23 initials and 36 finals. Many of those sounds bear some resemblance to English sounds. There are only a handful of Chinese sounds which are peculiar to Western ears. Don't be discouraged by

7

them – listen to them repeatedly and gradually you'll be able to pronounce them. Below is a full list of initials and finals with the closest equivalent sound in English wherever possible. Those which differ significantly from English sounds have explanations next to them.

Initials

f, l, m, n, s, w, y	similar to English
p, t, k	like *p* in *poor*, *t* in *tar* and *k* in *kite*
b, d	(more abrupt than their English equivalents) like *p* in *spend*, and *t* in *stamp*
g	like *g* in *girl*
h	like *h* in *hole* (but with a little friction in the throat)
j	like *g* in *George* (but with the tongue nearer the teeth)
q	a bit like *ch* in *cheese* (but with the tongue further forward)
z	like *ds* in *loads*
c	like *ts* in *toasts*
r	a bit like *r* in *run* (but with the tongue loosely rolled in the middle of the mouth)
zh	like *j* in *jail* (but with the tongue further back)
ch	a bit like *ch* in *chair* (but with the tongue further back and the mouth in a round shape)
sh	like *sh* in *short*
x	a bit like *sh* in *sheep* (the front of the tongue lies behind the lower front teeth, the tongue is in a relaxed position, and the mouth is in its natural shape – now try to whistle)

Finals

a	like *a* in *father*
ai	like *igh* in *high* but with a narrower mouth shape
ao	like *ow* in *how*
an	like *an* in *ban*

ang	like *on* in *monster*
e	like *ur* in *fur*
ei	like *ay* in *bay*
en	like *en* in *tent*
eng	**en** plus the strong nasal sound, a bit like *un* in *hunger*
er	*ur* in *fur* (with the tongue rolled back)
i	like *ea* in *tea* (but when **i** is preceded by **z**, **c**, **s**, **zh**, **ch**, **sh** and **r**, it simply functions as a helper to make those sounds audible and it is treated as a separate final)
ia	combine **i** and **a**
iao	like *eow* in *meow*
ie	like *ye* in *yes*
iu	like *you*
ian	similar to the Japanese currency word *yen*
in	like *in* in *bin*
iang	like *young*
ing	like *ing* in *outing*
iong	combine **i** with **ong**
o	like *ore* in *more*
ou	like *oa* in *toast*
ong	rather like *ong* in *ding-dong*
u	like *oo* in *boot*
ua	combine **u** with **a**
uo	like *war*
uai	combine **u** with **ai**
ui	like *wai* in *waiting*
uan	like *one*
un	a bit like *won* in *wonder*
uang	like *wan* in *wanting*
ü	like the French *u* in *tu*
üe	combine **ü** with a short **ei**

üan	combine ü with a short an
ün	a bit like *une* in French

▌ When initials do not precede **u** at the beginning of a syllable, **w** replaces **u**, e.g. **wang** instead of **uang**, **wo** instead of **uo**.

▌ When **ü** follows **j**, **q**, **x** and **y**, it is written as **u** without the two dots over it, but is still pronounced as **ü** because **u** never occurs after these initials, e.g. **ju** and **qu**, NOT **jü** and **qü**.

▌ The apostrophe (') is used to separate two syllables whenever there may be confusion over the syllable boundary. For example, in **shi'er** (twelve), **shi** is one syllable and **er** is another; in **chang'an** (long peace), **g** belongs to the first syllable not the second.

Tones

▌ One unique feature of the Chinese language is its tones. Every syllable in isolation is given a specific tone which helps to distinguish the meaning. Many words with exactly the same pronunciation but different tones mean completely different things. For example, **tang** in its high-level tone means 'soup' while in its rising tone it means 'sugar'. Don't be put off by this – even if you use the wrong tone, the context, your facial expression and many other things will help to put the message across.

▌ In **Putonghua** (Mandarin) there are four basic tones:

NAME		TONE MARK
First tone	(high-level)	ˉ
Second tone	(rising)	´
Third tone	(falling-rising)	˅
Fourth tone	(falling)	`

▌ In terms of an average person's voice range, the four tones can be visually represented like this:

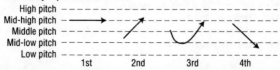

| | 1st | 2nd | 3rd | 4th |

High pitch
Mid-high pitch
Middle pitch
Mid-low pitch
Low pitch

In addition to the four basic tones above, there is a neutral tone. Syllables with neutral tones carry no specific tones and they are pronounced very weakly. If there is no tone mark over the vowel, the syllable must be a neutral tone. Try applying the tones to these syllables:

mā	má	mǎ	mà	ma
(mother)	(linen)	(horse)	(to swear)	[question word]

tāng	táng	tǎng	tàng
(soup)	(sugar)	(to lie down)	(boiling hot)

Please note that tones do change because of their surrounding tones. The three most common changes are:

i) When two third tones are together in the same meaning group, the first third tone changes to the second tone, e.g. nǐ, hǎo → Ní hǎo (Hello).

ii) When bù (not) is followed by another fourth tone, it changes to the second tone, e.g. bù, shì → Bú shì (No).

iii) The number word yī (one) has the first tone when used in isolation or at the end of a word or phrase, e.g. yī (one) and shí'yī (eleven); yī changes to the second tone when preceding fourth tones, e.g. yí liàng chē (one car); and yī changes to the fourth tone when preceding all the other three tones, e.g. yì běn shū (one book), yì jīn píngguǒ (one jin of apples), yì tóu niú (one cow). However, some people do use the first tone for yī all the time.

In this book, all the phrases in **pinyin** that occur in the main sections are marked with tones which reflect the tone changes (i.e. how they are actually pronounced in connected speech) except yi (when used to mean 'one') which remains the first tone throughout in this book to avoid confusion. The words listed in the English-Chinese Dictionary are marked with tones as if each syllable were in isolation. For example, the phrase ni hao in the relevant section is marked ní hǎo but in the Dictionary it is marked nǐ hǎo.

▌ Before you start learning Chinese, it is a good idea to know a few things about its grammar in order to facilitate your learning process.

Nouns and articles

▌ Nouns in Chinese have no singular and plural distinctions. Thus you say **yī běn *shū*** (one book) and **shí běn *shū*** (ten books).

▌ There are no articles in Chinese such as 'a' and 'the' in English. Thus **Wǒ qù mǎi shù** can mean 'I'm going to buy *a* book' or 'I'm going to buy *the* book'. The context helps to clarify the meaning.

Verbs

Forms

▌ As a consequence of the above principle, verbs (i.e. doing words) have only one form. For example, **qù** means 'to go to' and it is used in **Wǒ qù Lúndūn** (I go to London), **Tā qù Lúndūn** (He goes to London), **Wǒmen qù Lúndūn** (We go to London), etc.

Tenses

▌ Verbs do not change their forms to indicate past, present, future or continuous.

▌ The past tense is usually indicated by the past particle **le**, which is placed after the verb. For example:

Tā qù *le* Lúndūn.   (He went to London)

The above sentence can also be translated as 'He has gone to London', depending on the context.

❚ If you want to indicate a specific time in the past when a certain event took place, put the past particle **de** after the verb or at the end of the sentence:

Wó wǔ nián qián lái *de* Yīngguó   (I came to Britain five years ago)

Lit. I   five years ago   came   Britain

❚ If you want to say that you have experienced something or you have been somewhere, place the particle **guo** after the verb:

Wǒ qù *guo* Zhōngguó   (I have been to China)

❚ However, the above particles are never used together with the static verb **shì** (be). Whether it is present or past depends on time expressions and the context:

Sān nián qián   tā   *shì*   dǎoyóu   (He was a tourist guide three

Lit. Three years ago   he   be   tourist guide   years ago)

❚ The future tense is usually indicated by time phrases or placing **yào** before the verb:

Wǒ *míngnián*   qù Zhōngguó   (I'm going to China next year)

Lit. I   next year   go China

Wǒ *yào* qù Zhōngguó   (I'm going to China)

❚ The continuous tense is indicated by the continuous particle **zài** or **zhèngzài**, which is placed before the verb:

Wǒ *zài / zhèngzài* kàn diànshì   (I am watching TV)

The above sentence could also mean 'I was watching TV' if it were set in the past context.

Negation

❚ When you negate a sentence in English, you put 'do not', 'does not', 'did not', etc. before the verb. In Chinese, you simply put the negation word before the verb. There are two negation words: **bù** and **méi**.

■ **Bù** is used in most sentences. For example:

Tā	**bù**	**xǐhuan**	**Zhōngguó fàn**	(He doesn't like Chinese food)
Lit.	He	not	like	Chinese food

■ **Méi** is used to negate i) the verb **yǒu** (to have); and ii) things that have not happened or did not happen:

Wǒ	**méi**	**yǒu**	**Zhōngguó chá**	(I don't have Chinese tea)
Lit.	I	not	have	Chinese tea

Tā	**méi**	**qù**	**Zhōngguó**	(He didn't go/hasn't gone to China)
Lit.	He	not	go	China

Adjectives and adverbs

■ Adjectives (describing words) are placed before nouns, for example, *hǎo* **shū** (good book). Please note that **de** is inserted between an adjective and a noun if i) an adverb is placed before the adjective, for example, *hén hǎo de* **shū** (very good book); and ii) the adjective used consists of two syllables, for example, *piàoliang de* **shū** (beautiful book).

■ Some adjectives in Chinese can incorporate the verb 'to be', for example, **xiǎo** means 'small' in *xiǎo* **chéng** (*small* town) but 'to be small' in **Nǐde fángjiān** *xiǎo* (Your room *is small*). Do remember that the verb **shì** (to be) is not used in such cases. When adjectives are used for the above purpose, they are usually modified by adverbs such as **hěn** (very), **tǐng** (rather), **tài** (too), etc. For example, **Nǐde fángjiān** *tǐng* **xiǎo** (Your room is rather small).

■ Some adverbs share the same form as adjectives, for example, **hǎo** is an adjective in *hǎo* **shū** (good book) but an adverb in **shuì de** *hǎo* (slept well). Adverbs are sometimes placed before verbs in imperative sentences (i.e. ordering, suggesting), for example, **kuài** (quickly), in *Kuài* **chī** (Eat quickly).

Measure words

■ In English, only certain nouns are modified by this category of words, such as 'piece' in 'a piece of cake', 'pair' in 'a pair of trousers', etc. Just imagine that every noun in Chinese, when preceded by a number or a demonstrative pronoun (e.g. 'this', 'that') must have one of those words inserted between the number or demonstrative pronoun and the noun. These words are called 'measure words'. Different measure words are used with different nouns. For example, **běn** is used in **sān běn shū** (three books), **liàng** is used in **sān liàng chē** (three cars). More serious learners should try to match the right measure words with the right nouns. Below are some of the most commonly used measure words:

Pīnyīn	Category	Nouns (e.g.)
bāo	parcel, packet	books, biscuits
bēi	cup, glass	coffee, beer
běn	volume	dictionary, books
gè	people	man, girl
jiā	organisation	company, shop
kuài	square piece	soap, cake
liàng	things with wheels	bike, car
píng	bottle, jar	beer, jam
tiáo	long and winding	river, fish
tóu	big animals	pig, cow
zhāng	thin, flat	paper, ticket
zhī	small animals	chicken, duck
zuò	solid	mountain, house

■ To get by in Chinese, the measure word **gè** can be used in most circumstances, so you will be understood if you say, for example, **sān ge shū** instead of **sān běn shū**. Like most grammar rules, there are always exceptions. Measure words are not used in front of **tiān** (day), **nián** (year), etc. Thus you say **sān tiān** (three days), **yī nián** (one year), for example.

Word order

▌ Word order in Chinese is not too different from English. The common patterns are:

   subject + verb + object

   Wó   mǎi   shū   (I buy book)

subject + specific time + verb + object

Tā   liù diǎn   chī   wǎnfàn (She has supper at six o'clock)

subject + verb + a period of time + object

Tā   kàn le   yī ge xiǎoshí   diànshì (He watched TV for an hour)

subject + place   +   verb (+ object)

Wǒ   zài Běijīng   gōngzuò   (I work in Beijing)

object + subject + verb (to emphasise the object)

Xìn   wó   xiě le   (I did write the letter)

Questions

▌ When you ask a specific question regarding what, when, where, whom, etc., the sentence order is the same as that of a statement:

        Nǐ   jiào   shénme?   (What's your name?)

Lit.   You   are called   what?

        Nǐ   qù   nǎr?   (Where are you going?)

Lit.   You   go   where?

▌ When you ask a 'Yes' or 'No' question (e.g. Do you like it?/Are you Chinese?), all you need to do is to add the question word **ma** to the end of a sentence:

        Tā   shì   Zhōngguórén *ma*?   (Is she Chinese?)

Lit.   She   is   Chinese   [question word]?

Yes and No

■ The Chinese equivalents for 'yes' and 'no' are **shì de** and **bú shì** but they are not used as extensively as in English. In English, the standard answers to questions such as 'Do you like Chinese food?' are 'Yes, I do' or 'No, I don't', while in Chinese you usually repeat the verb in the question to mean 'Yes' and add the negative word before the verb to mean 'No':

    Nǐ *xǐhuan* Zhōngguó fàn   ma?   (Do you like Chinese food?)

Lit. You like   Chinese food   [question word]?

    ***Xǐhuan* / *Bù* xǐhuan**   (Yes, I do / No, I don't)

Lit.   Like / Not like

■ People will understand you if you reply with **Shì de** (Yes) or **Bú shì** (No) even though the reply is not good Chinese.

Understanding Chinese characters

■ Written Chinese is believed to be among the world's oldest written languages. Many of the earliest writings looked like pictures, known as pictographs. Gradually, the picture-like symbols have evolved into characters formed of strokes, and the structures have become more systemised and simpler. For example, the character for 'the sun' used to look like this: ⊙, and now it looks like this: 日.

■ There are about 50,000 Chinese characters, of which 3000 are used for everyday purposes such as in newspapers and menus.

■ There is little correlation between how characters are pronounced and how they are written. For example, the following three characters, consisting of very different strokes, are all pronounced **da** although with different tones: 大 dà, 打 dǎ, 答 dá. If you can read characters, tones become much less important in distinguishing the meaning. Therefore someone who can read both **pinyin** and characters finds it much easier to understand characters than **pinyin**.

■ There are some basic strokes on which many other combinations are based. A stroke is a single unbroken line. The basic strokes are:

一	horizontal stroke – from left to right
∣	vertical stroke – from top to bottom
✓	left-falling dot – from right to bottom left
ヽ	right-falling dot – from left to bottom right
ノ	left-falling – from top right to bottom left
﹨	right-falling – from top left to bottom right
／	rising – from bottom left to top right
⅃ L ∟	hook – all downward first, then make a hook
ㄱ ㄱ	turning – all from left to right first, then make a turning

▌ In writing a character, you are supposed to adhere to the following rules regarding stroke order:

Rule	Example	Stroke order	English
First horizontal, then vertical	十	一 十	ten
First left, then right	八	丿 八	eight
First left-falling, then right-falling	人	丿 人	person
First top, then bottom	三	一 二 三	three
First outside, then inside	问	门 问	to ask
First inside, then close	国	冂 囯 国	country
First middle, then left, then right	小	亅 亅 小	small/little

▌ Remembering the total number of strokes and the order of strokes does help to recognise and distinguish characters. For example: 大 means 'big' (three strokes), and 天 means 'sky' (four strokes).

▌ The majority of the Chinese characters consists of two components – one is the so-called 'radical', which indicates the categorisation of characters, and the other is called the 'phonetic', which provides some sort of clue to the pronunciation. For example, the character 清, pronounced **qīng** (meaning 'pure, clear'), consists of two components: the left 氵 is called the 'water radical', and the right part 青 gives the pronunciation **qing**. In other words, you need to remember each radical's name and how to write it first, and you also need to know how the other part is pronounced before it can function as a phonetic. Below are a few of the most commonly used radicals and their names:

Radicals	English	Name in Pinyin
亻	person	**rén zì páng**
女	woman	**nǚ zì páng**
艹	grass	**cǎo zì tóu**
口	mouth	**kǒu zì páng**
火 灬	fire	**huǒ zì páng**
讠	speech	**yán zì páng**

▌ In mainland China, about 2000 characters have been simplified, that is to say, some strokes have been either omitted or replaced with simpler strokes. For example, the simplified form for 車 is 车 (meaning 'car'). The traditional form, or 'complex form' is used in Hong Kong, Taiwan and other overseas Chinese communities. In this book, whenever there are two versions, the simplified version is introduced.

■ Calligraphy has always been regarded as a form of art in Chinese culture. In the old days, a scholar was no scholar if he was not an expert in music, chess, calligraphy and painting.

■ Do not worry about learning characters as a beginner. In this book, characters are only introduced for important signs. If you are really interested in learning characters, you can make some flash cards. Each card has a character on one side and the English translation and **pinyin** on the other. It will take you some time before you learn your first two hundred characters, but after that, you will notice that you progress faster and faster.

General phrases

▌ **Ní hǎo** (*lit.* you good/well), a general expression for 'hello', is used throughout the day. **Zǎoshang hǎo** (*lit.* Morning good) or simply **zǎo** is used, but not as extensively as 'Good morning' is in English. The Chinese equivalents of 'Good afternoon' and 'Good evening' are rarely used at all. Among friends, especially neighbours, typical greetings include **Chī le ma?** (Have you eaten?); **Shàng nǎr?** (Where are you going?); and **Huílai le** (You're back).

▌ Shake hands when you meet a Chinese person for the first time or when you see someone you haven't seen for a long time. However, keep your physical contact with Chinese people to the minimum as hugging and kissing in public are not appropriate and will embarrass the person concerned.

▌ Chinese people do not say 'Good night' to each other; they usually say the equivalent of 'I'll go to bed now'. However, it is perfectly acceptable for an English speaker to use the expression **Wǎn ān** (*lit.* evening peace).

▌ Chinese people tend to consider it immodest to accept personal compliments. For example, the likely response to 'Your English is very good' is 'Not good, not good'. However, attitudes are changing and some people nowadays do say 'Thank you' in response to compliments. Paying compliments to someone's children or home will be very welcome. 'Thank you' and 'Sorry' are not used as extensively as they are in many other languages, so don't feel offended if you don't hear them when they are expected.

Useful words

I/me	wǒ	their/theirs	tāménde
you (singular)	nǐ/nín (polite form)	a little	yìdiǎnr
		some	yìxiē
he/him	tā	OK/Good	Hǎo de
she/her	tā	not good	Bù hǎo
we/us	wǒmen	yes	shì de
you (plural)	nǐmen	(see BASIC GRAMMAR for its use)	
they/them	tāmen	no	bú shì
my/mine	wǒde	(see BASIC GRAMMAR for its use)	
your/yours	nǐde	not	bù/méi (yǒu)
his/hers	tāde	can't	bú huì
your/yours (plural)	nǐménde	do not have …	méi yǒu …
our/ours	wǒménde		

You may want to say

Greetings and goodbyes

Hello	Nǐ hǎo
Very pleased to meet you	Hěn gāoxìng jiàndào nǐ
Me too	Wǒ yě shì
Good morning	Zǎoshang hǎo
Are you well?	Nǐ hǎo ma?
How are you/things?	Zěnme yàng?
Fine, thanks	Hǎo, xièxie
Not bad, thanks	Bú cuò, xièxie
And you?	Nǐ ne?
Good night	Wǎn ān

Let's go	*Wǒmen zǒu ba*
Goodbye	*Zàijiàn*
See you later	*Huí jiàn*
See you tomorrow	*Míngtiān jiàn*

Communication problems

Can you speak …?	*Nǐ huì shuō … ma?*
… English	*… Yingwén …*
… standard Chinese (Mandarin)	*… Pǔtōnghuà …*
I can speak a little Chinese	*Wǒ huì shuō yìdiǎnr Zhōngwén*
My Chinese is very poor	*Wǒde Zhōngwén hěn bù hǎo*
I don't understand	*Wǒ bù dǒng*
I understand	*Wǒ dǒng le*
I don't know	*Wǒ bù zhīdào*
Could you repeat that?	*Nǐ kéyǐ zài shuō yí biàn ma?*
Slowly, please	*Qǐng màn yìdiǎnr*
How do you say … in Chinese?	*Zhōngwén zěnme shuō …?*
What does this/that mean?	*Zhè/Nà shì shénme yìsi?*
Just a moment, let me …	*Děngdeng, ràng wǒ …*
… think	*… xiǎngxiang*
… check the dictionary	*… chácha zìdiǎn*

Expressing gratitude and emotions

Thank you	*Xièxie*
Thank you very much	*Tài xièxie le*
You are so kind	*Nǐ tài hǎo le*
Thank you for your …	*Xièxie nǐde …*
… hospitality	*… zhāodài*
… present	*… lǐwù*
You're welcome	*Bú kèqi/Bú xiè*

I'm very ...	Wó hěn ...
... happy	... gāoxìng
... angry	... shēngqì
... worried/anxious	... zhāojí
I'm a bit ...	Wǒ yǒu yìdiǎnr ...
... tired	... lèi
... homesick	... xiǎng jiā (lit. miss home)

Apologising

I'm sorry	Duìbùqǐ
It doesn't matter/It's all right	Méi guānxi
Sorry I'm late	Duìbùqǐ, wǒ chí dào le
Excuse me	Duìbùqǐ/Láojià
Many apologies	Zhēn bàoqiàn
Please forgive me	Qǐng yuánliàng wǒ

Good wishes

Happy New Year	Xīn nián hǎo
Happy Birthday	Shēngrì kuàilè
Good luck	Hǎo yùnqi
Good health	Shēntǐ jiànkāng
Have a good time	Hǎohao wánr
Have a good journey	Yílù shùnfēng
Take care	Duō bǎozhòng

Weather

The weather's very good	Tiānqì hén hǎo
The weather's bad	Tiānqì bù hǎo
The weather's fine	Tiānqì bú cuò
It's sunny today	Jīntiān shì qíngtiān

It's fairly hot	*Tǐng rè de*
It's fairly cool	*Tǐng liángkuai*
It's very cold	*Hén lěng*
It's raining	*Xià yǔ le*
It's snowing	*Xià xuě le*
It's windy	*Qǐ fēng le*

You may hear

Huānyíng nǐ lái Zhōngguó	Welcome to China
Nǐ huì shuō Zhōngwén ma?	Can you speak Chinese?
Wǒ bú huì shuō Yīngwén	I can't speak English
Nǐ yílù shùnlì ma?	Did you have a good journey?
Nǐ lèi ma?	Are you tired?
Dǒng le ma?	Do you understand?
Qǐng hē chá	Please have some tea
Qǐng zuò	Please sit down
Qǐng chī	Please help yourself (*lit.* please eat)
Bié kèqi	Don't stand on ceremony
Nǐde Zhōngwén hén hǎo	Your Chinese is very good
Náli, náli/Guòjiǎng, guòjiǎng	Not at all

Talking about yourself and others

▌ In China family names or surnames are placed before given names. Titles, when used, are placed either at the very end or after family names. Family names contain only one syllable, while given names consist of one or two syllables. In the names **Wáng Tāo** and **Lǐ Fúlín** for example, **Wáng** and **Lǐ** are the family names and **Tāo** and **Fúlín** are given names. Some Chinese people living overseas have reversed the order of their names to avoid complications. The most common Chinese family names include **Wáng**, **Zhāng**, **Lǐ**, **Zhào**, **Sūn**, etc.

▌ The most common way of addressing a Chinese person is to use his or her full name. In mainland China, colleagues and friends sometimes address each other by putting **lǎo** (old) or **xiǎo** (young/little) in front of the family name, depending on the relative age and seniority of the speaker. Given names are used among families and friends. Some Chinese people use official names at school or work and completely different names at home and among family friends.

▌ Titles such as **xiānsheng** (Mr.) and **xiǎojie** (Miss) are used increasingly in business and tourist circles. The term **xiǎojie** is usually used for women under 40 regardless of marital status. For example, if a woman is called **Zhāng Lányīng**, she can be addressed and referred to as **Zhāng xiǎojie**. For women above 40, the term **nǚshì** (Madam) is sometimes used. The terms **xiānsheng** and **xiǎojie** can also be used on their own as a polite way of addressing strangers in places like hotels and restaurants (see BUSINESS TRIPS for professional titles).

▌ Chinese women in mainland China do not change their family names after they get married.

▌ Don't be offended if a Chinese person asks about your age and marital status as these are perceived as friendly questions.

▌ The term **àiren** (*lit.* love person) is commonly used in mainland China by a husband or wife to refer to his or her spouse, or used by other people to refer to someone else's husband or wife. Other terms for 'wife' and 'husband' are: **tàitai** (wife) and **xiānsheng** (husband), popular in Hong Kong, Taiwan and other overseas Chinese communities; and **qīzi/fūren** (wife) and **zhàngfu** (husband), which are more formal terms.

Useful words

what	*shénme*	Miss	*xiǎojie*
how	*zěnme*	whereabouts	*nǎli*
how old	*duō dà le*	where	*nǎr*
Mr.	*xiānsheng*	who	*shéi/shuí*

You may want to say

Names and ages

What's your family name? (*lit.* your honourable surname)?	*Nǐ xìng shénme?/Nín guì xìng*
My family name is Brown	*Wǒ xìng Brown*
What's ... name?	*... jiào shénme?*
... your ...	*Nǐ ...*
... his ...	*Tā ...*
... your friend's ...	*Nǐde péngyou ...*
My name is David Brown (*lit.* I am called ...)	*Wǒ jiào David Brown*
What shall I call you?	*Wǒ yìnggāi jiào nǐ shénme?*
Please call me David	*Qǐng jiào wǒ David*
Could you tell me what he is called?	*Nǐ kéyǐ gàosu wǒ tā jiào shénme ma?*
Sorry, I don't know his name	*Duìbùqǐ, wǒ bù zhīdào tāde míngzi*
I am Jane Smith	*Wǒ shì Jane Smith*

Are you …?	Nǐ shì … ma?
… Mr. Li	… Lǐ xiānsheng …
… Miss Chen	… Chén xiǎojie …
… Wang Lin's wife	… Wáng Lín de àiren/tàitai …
… Zhang Lan's husband	… Zhāng Lán de àiren/xiānsheng …
Who is he/she?	Tā shì shéi?
Let me introduce …	Ràng wǒ jièshào yíxià
How old are you?	Nǐ duō dà le?
(addressing a child)	Nǐ jǐ suì le?
(addressing an elderly or older person)	Nín jīnnián gāoshòu?
How old is she/he?	Tā duō dà le?
I am … years old	Wǒ … suì
… 29 …	… èrshíjiǔ
… 56 …	… wǔshíliù
He/She is … years old	Tā … suì
… 8 …	… bā …
… 10 …	… shí …

Nationalities

Where do you come from?	Nǐ cóng nǎr lái?
I come from …	Wǒ cóng … lái
… Britain	… Yīngguó …
… the United States	… Měiguó …
… Ireland	… Ài'ěrlán …
… Canada	… Jiānádà …
… Australia	… Àodàlìyà …
… New Zealand	… Xīnxīlán …
What's your nationality?	Nǐ shì nǎ guó rén?
(*lit.* You are which country person?)	
I am …	Wǒ shì …
… British	… Yīngguórén
… American	… Měiguórén

... Irish	... Ài'ěrlánrén
... Canadian	... Jiānádàrén
... Australian	... Àodàlìyàrén
... a New Zealander	... Xīnxīlánrén
Are you ...?	Nǐ shì ... ma?
... Japanese	... Rìběnrén ...
... Chinese	... Zhōngguórén ...
... Korean	... Cháoxiānrén ...
Which part of the country do you come from?	Nǐ shì nǎli rén?

Occupations

What do you do?	Nǐ gàn shénme gōngzuò?
I am ...	Wǒ shì ...
... a telephone receptionist	... diànhuà jiēxiànyuán
... a shop assistant	... shòuhuòyuán
... a doctor	... yīshēng/dàifu
... a nurse	... hùshi
... a lecturer	... jiǎngshī
... a teacher	... lǎoshī
... a businessperson	... shāngrén
... a salesman/saleswoman	... tuīxiāoyuán
... a writer	... zuòjiā
... an artist	... yìshùjiā
... a journalist	... jìzhě
... a lawyer	... lǜshī
... an actor/actress	... yǎnyuán
... painter	... huàjiā
... an engineer	... gōngchéngshī
... a mechanic	... jìshī
... a manual worker	... gōngrén

... a taxi driver	... *chūzūchē sījī*
... a secretary	... *mìshū*
... a student	... *xuésheng*
... a waiter/waitress	... *fúwùyuán*
I'm no longer working	*Wǒ bù gōngzuò le*
I'm retired	*Wǒ tuìxiū le*
I study ...	*Wǒ xuéxí ...*
... history	... *lìshǐ ...*
... chemistry	... *huàxué*

Family and friends

This is my ...	*Zhè shì wǒde ...*
... wife	... *tàitai/fūren*
... husband	... *xiānsheng*
... son	... *érzi*
... daughter	... *nǚ'ér*
... good friend	... *hǎo péngyou*
... boyfriend	... *nán péngyou*
... girlfriend	... *nǚ péngyou*
Are you married?	*Nǐ jiéhūn le ma?*
Yes, I am	*Jié le*
No, I'm not	*Méi jié*
I'm married	*Wǒ jiéhūn le*
I'm not married	*Wǒ méi jiéhūn*
Is that your ...?	*Nà shì nǐde ... ma?*
... mother	... *māma*
... father	... *bàba*
Do you have any children?	*Nǐ yǒu háizi ma?*
Yes, I do	*Yǒu*
No, I don't	*Méi yǒu*
How many children do you have?	*Nǐ yǒu jǐ ge háizi?*

What's your ... name?	... jiào shénme?
... son's ...	Nǐde érzi ...
... daughter's ...	Nǐde nǚ'er ...
Do you have any brothers and sisters?	Nǐ yǒu xiōngdì jiěmèi ma?
I have ...	Wó yǒu ...
... an elder sister	... yī ge jiějie
... a younger brother	... yī ge dìdi
I don't have any ...	Wǒ méi yǒu ...
... elder brothers	... gēge
... younger sisters	... mèimei
My parents live in London	Wǒde fùmǔ zhù zài Lúndūn
How is your ...?	Nǐde ... zěnme yàng?
... wife	... tàitai ...
... father	... bàba ...
Please give my regards to ...	Qǐng wèn ... hǎo
... your parents	... nǐde fùmǔ
... your elder sister	... Nǐde jiějie

Talking about China and your own country

I like ... (very much)	Wǒ (hén) xǐhuan ...
... China ...	... Zhōngguó
... Guilin ...	... Guìlín
... Chinese people ...	... Zhōngguórén
I don't like Chinese breakfast	Wǒ bù xǐhuan Zhōngguó zǎofàn
Do you like it?	Nǐ xǐhuan ma?
Do you like ...?	Nǐ xǐhuan ... ma?
... Chinese food	... Zhōngguó fàn ...
... cycling	... qí zìxíngchē ...
This place is ...	Zhè ge dìfang ...
... interesting	... yǒu yìsi/ hǎo wánr

… boring	… méi yìsi/ bù hǎo wánr
… all right	… hái kěyǐ
Your … is lovely	Nǐde … hén kě'ài
… daughter …	… nǚ'ér …
… girlfriend …	… nǚ péngyou …
Your home is very nice	Nǐ jiā hěn bú cuò
I've fallen in love with China	Wǒ ài shang le Zhōngguó
China is very beautiful	Zhōngguó hén měi
Chinese people are very friendly	Zhōngguórén hěn yǒuhǎo
It's my first time in China	Zhè shì wǒ dì yī cì lái Zhōngguó
I often come to China	Wǒ cháng lái Zhōngguó
Have you been to …?	Nǐ qù guo … ma?
… Britain	… Yīngguó …
… America	… Měiguó
What do/did you think of …?	Nǐ juéde … zěnme yàng?
… London	… Lúndūn …
… New York	… Niǔyuē …

You may hear

Nǐ shì Smith xiānsheng ma?	Are you Mr. Smith?
Nǐ xìng Brown ma?	Is Brown your surname?
Nǐ jiào David ma?	Are you called David?
Jiào wǒ Xiáo Lǐ ba	Please call me Xiao Li
Nǐ kànshangqu hěn niánqīng	You look very young
Wǒ bú xìn	I don't believe it
Kàn bù chū	You don't look it (your age)
Nǐde háizi duō dà le?	How old are your children?
Tāmen shì nánhái háishì nǚhái?	Are they boys or girls?
Nǐ yǒu méi yǒu gēge?	Do you have any elder brothers?

Níde fùmǔ zhù zài nǎr?	Where do your parents live?
Wǒ shì ...	I am ...
... Shànghǎirén	... Shanghainese
... Běijīngrén	... Beijingnese
Zhè shì nǐ dì yī cì lái Zhōngguó ma?	Is this your first time in China?
Nǐ xǐhuan Zhōngguó zǎofàn ma?	Do you like Chinese breakfast?
Nǐ zài Zhōngguó dāi duō jiǔ?	How long are you staying in China?
Nǐ xué shénme (zhuānyè)?	What do you study?
Nǐ zhù zai Yīngguó shénme dìfang?	Whereabouts in Britain do you live?
Nǐ shì Měiguó nǎli rén?	Whereabouts in America do you come from?

Numbers

▪ Arabic numbers are widely used in China but numbers in Chinese script are often used as well, for instance on price tags in shops. Both Arabic numbers and numbers in Chinese script appear on Chinese banknotes and coins. For numbers, there are two sets of script, for example, '1' is represented by both '一' (simple set) and '壹' (complicated set). On banknotes and receipts, the complicated set is used together with Arabic numbers to avoid any possible confusion. Both sets of script for numbers from one to 10 are listed below.

▪ See BASIC GRAMMAR for how to use numbers with nouns.

▪ **Yī** and **yāo** both mean 'one'. **Yāo** is used instead of **yī** in number sequences, for example, in saying telephone numbers and bus and train numbers.

▪ **Èr** and **liǎng** both mean 'two'. **Èr** is used for counting and saying other numbers such as 'twenty-two', while **liǎng** is normally used to quantify things such as 'two books', 'two days', 'two hours', etc.

Cardinals

Arabic numbers	Pīnyīn	Characters	Characters (used in banknotes and receipts)
0	líng	零	零
1	yī	一	壹
2	èr	二	贰
3	sān	三	叁
4	sì	四	肆
5	wǔ	五	伍
6	liù	六	陆
7	qī	七	柒
8	bā	八	捌

9	*jiǔ*	九	玖
10	*shí*	十	拾

11	*shíyī* (lit. ten one)		
12	*shí'èr*	50	*wǔshí*
13	*shísān*	60	*liùshí*
14	*shísì*	70	*qīshí*
15	*shíwǔ*	80	*bāshí*
16	*shíliù*	90	*jiǔshí*
17	*shíqī*	100	*yī bǎi*
18	*shíbā*	101	*yī bǎi líng yī*
19	*shíjiǔ*		(lit. one hundred zero one)
20	*èrshí* (lit. two ten)	102	*yī bǎi líng èr*
21	*èrshíyī*	103	*yī bǎi líng sān*
22	*èrshí'èr*	110	*yī bǎi yīshí*
23	*èrshísān*	111	*yī bǎi yīshíyī*
24	*èrshísì*	112	*yī bǎi yīshí'èr*
25	*èrshíwǔ*	200	*èr bǎi*
26	*èrshíliù*	201	*èr bǎi líng yī*
27	*èrshíqī*	1000	*yī qiān*
28	*èrshíbā*	10,000	*yī wàn*
29	*èrshíjiǔ*	100,000	*shí wàn*
30	*sānshí*	1,000,000	*yī bǎi wàn*
40	*sìshí*	10,000,000	*yī qiān wàn*

Ordinals

1st	*dì yī*	6th	*dì liù*
2nd	*dì èr*	7th	*dì qī*
3rd	*dì sān*	8th	*dì bā*
4th	*dì sì*	9th	*dì jiǔ*
5th	*dì wǔ*	10th	*dì shí*

Fractions

$^1/_2$ èr fēnzhī yī $^1/_3$ sān fēnzhī yī $^1/_4$ sì fēnzhī yī. $^3/_4$ sì fēnzhī sān

Percentages

0.5 %   *bǎifēnzhī líng diǎn wǔ* (lit. percentages zero point five)
10 %   *bǎifēnzhī shí*
50 %   *bǎifēnzhī wǔshí*
100 %   *bǎifēnzhī bǎi*

Time and the calendar

■ Although China is a vast land, it operates on one standard time – Beijing Time, which is Greenwich Mean Time plus eight hours.

■ Once you know the numbers from one to 12, telling the time in Chinese is very easy. You tell the time in the following order: hour + **diǎn** (*lit.* point) + minute + **fēn** (minute), for example, **sān diǎn wǔ fēn** (five past three). Note that **liǎng** (two) is used instead of **èr** in **liáng diǎn** (two o'clock).

■ The 24-hour clock is used at airports, railway stations, on TV, etc.

■ The Western calendar is used for all official purposes but in the countryside peasants still prefer the lunar calendar as it is more practical for their agricultural time-table. In the lunar calendar, there are either 29 or 30 days in each month (28 days in February) so at the end of a third year there is a leap month (e.g. two Aprils or two Augusts) and before the end of the fifth year a second leap month will appear in the calendar. All the Chinese festivals are calculated according to the lunar calendar (see NATIONAL HOLIDAYS AND FESTIVALS). In Chinese calendars, the lunar calendar dates are printed below the Western calendar dates.

■ When giving a date, the year comes first, followed by the month, then the date.

Useful words

what time	*jǐ diǎn*	every day	*měi tiān*
what day	*xīngqī jǐ*	this morning	*jīntiān zǎoshang/shàngwǔ*
what date	*jǐ hào*	this afternoon	*jīntiān xiàwǔ*
today	*jīntiān*	tonight	*jīntiān wǎnshang*
yesterday	*zuótiān*	evening	*wǎnshang*
tomorrow	*míngtiān*	this week	*zhège xīngqī*

this month	*zhège yuè*	before	*cóngqián/ yǐqián*
last week	*shàngge xīngqī*	in future	*jiānglái*
last month	*shàngge yuè*	after	*… hòu*
next week	*xiàge xīngqī*	always	*zǒngshì*
next month	*xiàge yuè*	twenty minutes	*èrshí fēnzhōng*
every week	*měige xīngqī*	three hours	*sān ge xiǎoshí/zhōngtóu*
every month	*měige yuè*	five days	*wǔ tiān*
this year	*jīn nián*	two weeks	*liǎng ge xīngqī*
last year	*qù nián*	one month	*yī ge yuè*
next year	*míng nián*	weekend	*zhōumò*
now	*xiànzài*		

You may want to say

Telling the time

What time is it, please?	*Qǐng wèn, jǐ diǎn le?*
It's …	
… one o'clock	*Yī diǎn*
… two o'clock	*Liǎng diǎn*
… 6 a.m.	*Zǎoshang/Shàngwǔ liù diǎn* (*lit.* morning 6 o'clock)
… 6 p.m.	*Wǎnshang liù diǎn* (*lit.* evening 6 o'clock)
… 12 midnight	*Bànyè shí'èr diǎn*
… 12 midday	*Zhōngwǔ shí'èr diǎn*
It's … past one	*Yī diǎn …*
… five …	*… wǔ fēn*
… a quarter …	*… yī kè*
… twenty …	*… èrshí fēn*
… half …	*… bàn*

It's one ...	Yī diǎn ...
... thirty	... sānshí fēn
... forty-five	... sìshíwǔ
It's ... to two	Liǎng diǎn
... five ...	... chà wǔ fēn (lit. missing five minutes)
... a quarter ...	... chà yī kè
... twenty-five ...	... chà èrshíwǔ

Asking about the time

Excuse me	Duìbùqǐ
What time is it, please?	Qǐng wèn, jǐ diǎn le?
What time is ...?	Jǐ diǎn ...?
... breakfast	... chī zǎofàn (lit. eat breakfast)
... lunch	... chī wǔfàn/zhōngfàn
... supper	... chī wǎnfàn
What time does the canteen ...?	Cāntīng jǐ diǎn ...?
... open	... kāimén
... close	... guānmén
How long does it take to get there?	Xūyào duō jiǔ kéyǐ dào?
What time does the Beijing Opera begin?	Jīngjù jǐ diǎn kāishǐ?
What time do you ...?	Nǐ jǐ diǎn ...?
... get up	... qǐchuáng
... have your breakfast	... chī zǎofàn
... go to bed	... shuìjiào

Days

As Monday is the first day of the week, it is **xīngqīyī**, which means 'week day one'. However, Sunday is not **xīngqīqī** (week day seven) but **xīngqītiān** (lit. week day heaven) or **xīngqīrì** (lit. week day sun).

What day is it today?	*Jīntiān shì xīngqī jǐ?*
Today is …	*Jīntiān shì …*
… Monday	*… xīngqīyī*
… Tuesday	*… xīngqī'èr*
… Wednesday	*… xīngqīsān*
… Thursday	*… xīngqīsì*
… Friday	*… xīngqīwǔ*
… Saturday	*… xīngqīliù*
… Sunday	*… xīngqītiān/xīngqīrì*

Months

If you imagine January is 1 and December is 12, for the month in Chinese simply add **yuè** after the numbers from 1 to 12:

I was born in …	*Wǒ chūshēng zài …*
… January	*… yīyuè*
… February	*… èryuè*
… March	*… sānyuè*
… April	*… sìyuè*
… May	*… wǔyuè*
… June	*… liùyuè*
… July	*… qīyuè*
… August	*… bāyuè*
… September	*… jiǔyuè*
… October	*… shíyuè*
… November	*… shíyīyuè*
… December	*… shí'èryuè*

Dates

Add **hào** after the number which indicates the date:

What's the date today?	*Jīntiān shì jǐ hào?*
Today is the …	*Jīntiān shì …*
… 1st	… *yī hào*
… 2nd	… *èr hào*
… 3rd	… *sān hào*
… 4th	… *sì hào*
… 11th	… *shíyī hào*
… 21st	… *èrshíyī hào*
It's the …	*Jīntiān shì …*
… 18th of March	… *sānyuè shíbā hào*
… 25th of May	… *wǔyuè èrshíwǔ hào*
… 6th October 1996	*yījiǔjiǔliù nián shíyuè liù hào*

Seasons

I like … most	*Wǒ zuì xǐhuan …*
… spring …	… *chūntiān*
… summer …	… *xiàtiān*
… autumn …	… *qiūtiān*
… winter …	… *dōngtiān*

Changing money

▌ Foreign currencies are not readily accepted in China, so converting your currency to Chinese **yuan** is a necessity. You can exchange foreign currency or traveller's cheques in the Bank of China, at foreign exchange counters in large hotels or at the airport, and in many Friendship Stores. Foreign exchange counters in large hotels are the easiest to find and also the most efficient to deal with. You may also find that they offer a better rate than the Bank of China.

▌ When exchanging foreign currency into Chinese **yuan**, you will be asked to produce your passport. You will also be given a receipt with details of the transaction. If by the end of your trip you have not spent all of your Chinese **yuan** and wish to change it back into the foreign currency, this receipt will allow you to do so.

▌ China is a cash-carrying society. It is only recently that credit cards such as American Express, Visa, Mastercard/Access etc. have been accepted by some large hotels. Cheques are used only by businesses in China and ordinary people do not have personal cheque-books, so it is a good idea to take enough cash with you if you go to a small town or village for the day.

▌ The formal name for Chinese currency is **Rénmín Bì** (*lit.* people's currency) and it is abbreviated as RMB with the sign ¥. The Foreign Exchange Certificate (FEC) system, which was invented in the late 70s to control foreign currencies (in those days, only FEC could be exchanged for foreign currencies), proved to be a mistake and has been abolished. Unlike in sterling where there are only two units, pounds and pence, in Chinese currency there are three units: **yuán**, **jiǎo** and **fēn**. The informal terms are: **kuài**, **máo** and **fēn**. Ten **fēn** make up one **jiǎo/máo** and 10 **jiǎo/máo** make up one **yuán/kuài**. So, if you see ¥1.54 as a price, it is read **yī yuán wǔ jiǎo sì (fēn)** or **yī kuài wǔ máo sì (fēn)**.

You may see

银行	yínháng	bank
外汇兑换	wàihuì duìhuàn	foreign exchange counter
人民币(元)	Rénmín Bì (yuán)	Chinese yuan
美元	Měi yuán	US dollar
英镑	Yīng bàng	sterling
法国法郎	Fǎguó fǎláng	French franc
德国马克	Déguó mǎkè	Deutschmarks
元/角/分	yuán/jiǎo/fēn	(currency units)
块/毛/分	kuài/máo/fēn (informal)	(currency units)

You may want to say

Where can I change money?	Wǒ kéyǐ zài nǎr huàn qián?
I'd like to change some ...	Wó xiǎng huàn yìxiē ...
... US dollars	... Měi yuán
... pounds	... Yīng bàng
... traveller's cheques	... lǚxíng zhīpiào
What's the exchange rate?	Duìhuàn lǜ shì duōshǎo?
Could I have a receipt, please?	Qǐng gěi wǒ yī zhāng shōujù, hǎo ma?
Could you change this for small coins?	Kéyǐ gěi wǒ huàn yìxiē líng qián ma?
Could I have 50 notes, please?	Kéyǐ gěi wǒ wǔshí yuán de chāopiào ma?
I'd like to change these yuan back into ...	Wǒ xiǎng bǎ zhèxiē Rénmín Bì huàn huí ...
... US dollars	... Měi yuán
... pounds	... Yīng bàng
Here is the receipt	Zhè shì wǒde shōujù

You may hear

Qǐng zài zhèr qiān míng	Please sign here
Kéyi kàn yíxià nǐde hùzhào ma?	Your passport, please?
Yì Yīng bàng duì shísān yuán	It's 13 *yuan* to the pound
Ní xiǎng huàn duōshǎo?	How much do you want to exchange?
Zhè shì nǐde shōujù	Here is your receipt
Duìbùqǐ, wǒmen bù shōu …	Sorry, we don't accept …
… zhīpiào	… cheques
… xìnyòng kǎ	… credit cards
Wǒmen zhǐ shōu xiànjīn	We only accept cash

Finding your way

■ Most Chinese cities are divided into four districts: East District, South District, West District and North District.

■ **Jiē** (streets) or **Dàjiē** (avenues) usually run from east to west, and **Lù** (roads) usually run from north to south. Small lanes are called **hútong** or **xiàng** in the north and **lǐlòng** in the south.

■ The centre of Beijing is Tian'anmen Square; most streets east of Tian'anmen Square have the prefix **dōng** attached to the street name. For example, the street right in front of Tian'anmen Square is called **Cháng'ān Dàjiē** (Forever Peace Avenue), and the avenue to the east of Tian'anmen Square is called **Dōng Cháng'ān Dàjiē** (East Forever Peace Avenue).

■ Instead of saying 'left' and 'right', Chinese people sometimes use **dōng** (east), **nán** (south), **xī** (west) and **běi** (north) when giving directions.

■ Chinese maps are not very user-friendly, but it is still a good idea to get a map so that you can ask the locals to mark out where you are and where you want to go. If you are looking for a residential address, it is a good idea to have the address written down in Chinese characters and to find out beforehand from the people who live there which district they live in and the most obvious building or famous organisation nearby. If you really get stuck, it is always a good idea to ask a traffic police officer; they are often to be found at major crossroads. Traffic policemen wear a green uniform in autumn and winter and a white uniform in spring and summer, both with yellow stripes on the cuffs.

■ Chinese people use the same system as Americans when it comes to numbering floors in a building. Thus the British ground floor would be **yī céng** (1st floor), and the first floor would be **èr céng** (2nd floor), and so on.

You may see

东/南/西/北	*dōng/nán/xī/běi*	east/south/west/north
街/大街/路	*Jiē/Dàjiē/Lù*	street/avenue/road
人行横道	*rénxíng héngdào*	pedestrian crossing
地下通道	*dìxià tōngdào*	underpass
禁止入内	*jìnzhǐ rù nèi*	no entry
进口	*jìnkǒu*	entrance
出口	*chūkǒu*	exit
厕所	*cèsuǒ*	toilet
男	*nán*	Men (toilet)
女	*nǚ*	Women (toilet)
胡同	*hútòng*	lane
巷	*xiàng*	lane
号	*hào*	number

Useful words

where	*nǎr/shénme dìfang*
Where is …?	*… zài nǎr*
How do I get to …?	*Qù … zěnme zǒu*
near	*jìn*
far	*yuǎn*
map	*dìtú*
left	*zuǒ*
right	*yòu*
upstairs	*lóushàng*
downstairs	*lóuxià*
straight ahead	*yìzhí zǒu*
next to	*zài … de páng biān*

behind	*zài ... de hòumian*
in front of	*zài ... de qiánmian*
opposite	*zài ... de duìmiàn*
traffic light	*hónglǜ dēng (lit. red green light)*

Excuse me, I'm lost	*Duìbùqǐ, wǒ mílù le*
Please point out where we are on the map	*Qǐng zài dìtú shang zhǐchū wǒmen zài nǎr*
Where is it on the map?	*Zài dìtú shang shénme dìfang?*
How do I get to ...?	*Qù ... zěnme zǒu?*
... the Friendship Store	*... Yǒuyì Shāngdiàn*
... the railway station	*... huǒchē zhàn*
... the Beijing Hotel	*... Běijīng Fàndiàn*
Where is ...?	*... zài nǎr?*
... the toilet	*Cèsuǒ ...*
... the post office	*Yóu jú ...*
Is this the correct way to ...?	*Zhè shì qù ... de lù ma?*
... the Forbidden City	*... Gùgōng ...*
... the Temple of Heaven	*... Tiāntán ...*
Is there a ... around here?	*Fùjìn yǒu ... ma?*
... bank ...	*... yínháng ...*
... public telephone ...	*... gōngyòng diànhuà ...*
How do I get there?	*Zěnme zǒu?*
Is it far?	*Yuǎn bù yuǎn?*
Can I walk there?	*Wǒ kéyǐ zǒulù qù ma?*
How long does it take to walk?	*Zǒulù yào zǒu duō jiǔ?*
Is there a bus going in that direction?	*Yǒu gōnggòng qìchē qù nà ge fāngxiàng ma?*

What ... is this?	*Zhè shì shénme ...?*
... district ...	*... qū*
... street ...	*... jiē*
Is this Yueya Lane?	*Zhè shì Yuèyá hútong ma?*
I'd like to buy a map of Xi'an	*Wǒ xiáng mǎi yi zhāng Xī'ān dìtú*

You may hear

Yìzhí zǒu	Go straight ahead
Wǎng ... guǎi	Turn ...
... yòu ...	... right
... dōng ...	... east
Dào hónglǜ dēng, wǎng xī guǎi	At the traffic light, turn west
Cèsuǒ zài ...	The toilet is ...
... lóushàng	... upstairs
... lóuxià	... downstairs
... èr céng	... on the first floor
Yínháng zài fàndiàn de ... biān	The bank is to the ... of the hotel
... zuǒ ...	... left ...
... yòu ...	... right ...
Fàndiàn zài yínháng de ...	The hotel is ... the bank
... hòumian	... behind ...
... duìmiàn	... opposite ...
Hěn jìn, zǒulù shí fēnzhōng	Very close, 10 minutes' walk
Duìmiàn nà ge lóu jiù shì	It's that building opposite us
Zhè jiù shì	This is it
Nǐ zhǎo jǐ hào?	What number are you looking for?

▋ All passenger trains in China are numbered. In general, trains with one or two digits are fast trains, while those with three digits are usually slow trains.

▋ On long-distance trains, you have three choices: soft-sleepers, hard-sleepers and hard-seats. Each soft-sleeper compartment contains four small berths (rather like two sets of bunk beds). Soft-sleepers are the most comfortable and thus the most expensive. Hard-sleeper berths are harder and have less space than soft-sleepers. There are upper, middle and lower berths. Upper berths are slightly cheaper but more cramped. The hard-seat carriages are extremely crowded and the seats are uncomfortable, so try to avoid travelling hard-seat. If you travel by hard-sleeper or hard-seat, you will need to bring your own cup to drink from. Hot water is supplied on the train. Note that smoking is allowed in all carriages.

▋ Between some big cities such as Beijing and Shanghai, there are several special express trains which stop only at major stations and have soft and comfortable chairs only.

▋ On all long-distance and medium-distance trains, there is a restaurant car where you can have a sit-down meal. Alternatively, you can buy boxes of food served at meal times from a trolley in each carriage.

▋ As demand for train tickets exceeds supply, always book your tickets at least three days before you travel. You can buy tickets through the travel office in your hotel or at the ticket office designated for foreigners at the railway station or at a ticket office in town.

▋ To buy a train ticket, you simply ask for the particular kind of seat you require (soft-sleeper, hard-sleeper or hard-seat), and state the train number (if you know it) or simply the destination and the day of travel. The following information is printed on a ticket: point of departure and destination, type of seat, carriage number and seat number, price, and how many days it is valid for. As you are allocated a seat number automatically, there is no seat reservation service. You cannot buy return tickets in China, so it is wise to sort out your next journey ticket as soon as you get to the destination.

■ You can break your journey as many times as you want, but the ticket is only valid for three to five days (as stated on the ticket). When you resume your journey, you can get on any train heading for the same destination; however, you lose your allocated seat and simply have to look for another seat after you get on the train.

■ Soft-sleeper ticket holders can use the **ruǎn wò hòuchē shì** (soft-sleeper waiting-room) which is more comfortable than ordinary waiting-rooms.

You may see

火车站	*huǒchē zhàn*	railway station
火车票	*huǒchē piào*	rail ticket
问询处	*wènxùn chù*	enquiries
外宾售票处	*wàibīn shòupiào chù*	ticket office for foreigners
软卧	*ruǎn wò*	soft-sleeper
硬卧	*yìng wò*	hard-sleeper
硬座	*yìng zuò*	hard-seat
站台	*zhàntái*	platform
行李寄存处	*xínglǐ jìcún chù*	left-luggage
软卧候车室	*ruǎn wò hòuchē shì*	soft-sleeper waiting-room
餐车	*cān chē*	dining car
发车/开车	*fāchē/kāichē*	departure
到站	*dàozhàn*	arrival
目的地	*mùdìdì*	destination
车次	*chē cì*	train number
车厢	*chē xiāng*	carriage/coach
厕所	*cèsuǒ*	toilet
出口	*chūkǒu*	way out

北京	*Běijīng*	Beijing / Peking
上海	*Shànghǎi*	Shanghai
西安	*Xī'ān*	Xi'an
广州	*Guǎngzhōu*	Guangzhou / Canton
桂林	*Guìlín*	Guilin
拉萨	*Lāsā*	Lhasa (in Tibet)
重庆	*Chóngqìng*	Chongqing / Chongking

Useful words

when	*shénme shíhou*	where	*nǎr/shénme dìfang*
what time	*jǐ diǎn*	how long	*duō jiǔ*
which train	*nǎ tàng chē*	Is there ...?	*Yǒu ... ma?*
which platform	*nǎge zhàntái*		

You may want to say

Information

Is there a train to Chongqing?	*Yǒu qù Chóngqìng de huǒchē ma?*
Is there an express train to Xi'an?	*Yǒu qù Xī'ān de tèkuài ma?*
Which number train can I take to go to Lhasa?	*Wǒ kéyi zuò ná jǐ cì chē qù Lāsā?*
What time does ... leave?	*... jǐ diǎn fāchē?*
... the No. 8 train ...	*Bā cì lièchē ...*
... the next train to Beijing ...	*Xià tàng qù Běijīng de chē ...*
... the first train to Shanghai ...	*Dì yī tàng qù Shànghǎi de chē ...*
... the last train to Xi'an ...	*Zuìhòu yī tàng qù Xī'ān de chē ...*
Does this train go to ...?	*Zhè tàng chē qù ... ma?*

What time does it arrive in …?	*Jí diǎn dào …?*
… Xi'an	*… Xī'ān*
… Chengdu	*… Chéngdū*
What time does the train from … arrive?	*Cóng … lái de chē jí diǎn dào?*
Do I have to change trains?	*Wǒ xūyào huàn chē ma?*
Where do I have to change?	*Wǒ xūyào zài nǎr huàn chē?*
How long does it take to get to …?	*Dào … xūyào duō jiǔ?*
Which platform is it for …?	*… shì jǐ zhàntái?*
Is this the right platform for No. … train?	*… cì chē shì zài zhège zhàntái ma?*
Does this train have air-conditioning?	*Zhè tàng lièchē yǒu kōngtiáo ma?*

Tickets

I'd like a ticket for …	*Wǒ xiáng mǎi yī zhāng … piào*
… an express train	*… tèkuài chē*
… a fast train	*… kuài chē*
… a slow train	*… màn chē*
… the No. 8 train	*… bā cì lièchē*
I'd like … please	*Wǒ xiáng mǎi yī zhāng …*
… a soft-sleeper …	*… ruǎn wò*
… a hard-sleeper …	*… yìng wò*
… a hard-seat …	*… yìng zuò*
… an upper berth …	*… shàng pù*
… a lower berth …	*… xià pù*
… an adult's ticket …	*… dàrén piào/chéngrén piào*
… a child's ticket …	*… xiǎohái piào/értóng piào*
One/two … to Xi'an, please	*Yī/liǎng zhāng qù Xī'ān de … .*
… soft-sleeper(s) …	*… ruǎn wò piào*
… hard-sleeper(s) …	*… yìng wò piào*
Are there any soft-sleeper tickets left for the No. 76 train?	*Hái yǒu qī shíliù cì lièchē de ruǎn wò piào ma?*

How much is it?	*Duō shǎo qián?*
I'd like to leave …	*Wǒ xiǎng … zǒu*
… on Monday	*… xīngqíyī*
… tomorrow	*… míngtiān*
… on Tuesday morning	*… xīngqí'èr zǎoshang …*

Left-luggage

Can I leave this/these here?	*Wǒ kéyǐ bǎ zhège/zhèxiē cún zài zhèr ma?*
What is the charge?	*Zěnme shōufèi?*
What time do you open?	*Nǐmen jǐ diǎn kāimén?*
What time do you close?	*Nǐmen jǐ diǎn guānmén?*

On the train

Is this the right train for …?	*Zhè shì qù … de chē ma?*
What is the next stop?	*Xià yī zhàn shì nǎr?*
How long does it take to get to …?	*Dào … xūyào duō jiǔ?*
… Guangzhou	*… Guǎngzhōu …*
… the next stop	*… xià yī zhàn …*
How long does this train stop here?	*Zhè liàng chē zài zhèr tíng duō jiǔ?*
Is there a restaurant car on this train?	*Zhè liàng chē shang yǒu cān chē ma?*
Where is the toilet?	*Cèsuǒ zài nǎr?*
Where are we now?	*Wǒmen xiànzài zài nǎr?*
What station is this?	*Zhè shì nǎ yī zhàn?*
Excuse me, this is my seat	*Duìbùqǐ, zhè shì wǒde zuòwèi*
Could you let me know when we get to …?	*Dào … de shíhou nǐ kéyǐ gàosù wǒ ma?*
… Guilin	*… Guìlín …*
… Guangzhou	*… Guǎngzhōu …*
What time are we due to arrive at …?	*Wǒmen jǐ diǎn dào …?*
May I open the window?	*Wǒ kéyǐ kāi chuānghu ma?*

May I switch off the light?	*Wǒ kéyǐ guān dēng ma?*
Excuse me, can I get past?	*Duìbùqǐ, wǒ kéyǐ guò yíxià ma?*
Could you keep an eye on this for me for a second?	*Nǐ bāng wǒ zhǎokàn yíxià zhège, xíng ma?*
I'd like to change to a soft-sleeper	*Wó xiǎng huàn chéng ruǎn wò*

You may hear

Information

Shíwǔ cì chē liù diǎn shí fēn fāchē	No. 15 train leaves at 6.10
Wǔ diǎn bàn dào	It arrives at 5.30
Nǐ yīnggāi zài … huàn chē	You should change at …
Jiǔshíyī cì chē cóng sān zhàntái fāchē	No. 91 train leaves from platform 3
Shíbā cì lièchē zài Wúxī bù tíng	No. 18 train does not stop at Wuxi

Tickets

Duìbùqǐ, xīngqíyī de piào mài guāng le	Sorry, Monday's tickets are sold out
Zhè tàng chē méi yǒu …	This train has no …
… ruǎn wò	… soft-sleepers
… kōngtiáo	… air-conditioning
Yìng wò xíng ma?	Will hard-sleeper be OK?
Nǐ shénme shíhou zǒu?	When are you leaving?
Nǐ xiǎng jí diǎn zǒu?	What time do you want to leave?
Jǐ zhāng piào?	How many tickets?

On the train

Nǐ gāi xiàchē le	This is your stop
Xià yī zhàn shì Guìlín	The next stop is Guilin
Huǒchē zài zhèr tíng shíwǔ fēnzhōng	The train stops here for 15 minutes

■ Air China, formerly known as CAAC (the Civil Aviation Administration of China), is the largest national airline and the only one which flies international routes. Air China also operates some domestic air services within China. In addition to Air China, there are many regional airlines, such as China Eastern Airlines, China Southeast Airlines and China Northwest Airlines; these operate internal flights only (see USEFUL ADDRESSES AND TELEPHONE NUMBERS). Air China provides one of the best services in China, with a superior fleet of aircraft and the best safety record.

■ Signs at most airports are printed in both Chinese and English. **Shǒudū jīchǎng** (Capital Airport) is the international airport in Beijing and **Hóngqiáo jīchǎng** (Hongqiao Airport) is the international airport in Shanghai.

■ You must pay airport departure tax on both international and domestic flights in Chinese **yuan**, so you should keep some cash for this purpose. You pay the departure tax before you check in. You will be given a receipt for this payment; keep it in a safe place as you need to show it to the airport staff before entering the check-in area.

■ Always check your departure gate near to the boarding time as it may change.

■ Only international airports such as Beijing, Shanghai and Guangzhou have Bank of China counters where you can change money.

■ Air tickets are sold at the airport, in ticket offices in town, and in luxury hotels. If you book your ticket(s) by phone, you must go to the office where you've made the booking to collect the ticket(s). You must then present the passport(s) of the passengers and pay for your ticket(s) in cash. Children over 12 years of age pay a full adult's fare.

■ In some large cities such as Beijing and Shanghai, there are airport buses running between the airport and the town centre. The service is regular and much cheaper than taxis. You can find out the details of these buses from the airline ticket office.

飞机场	fēijīchǎng	airport
问询处	wènxún chù	information desk
售票处	shòupiào chù	ticket office
国际	guójì	international
国内	guónèi	domestic
到港/到达	dàogǎng/dàodá	arrival
离港/离开	lígǎng/líkāi	departure
登机口	dēngjī kǒu	boarding gate
办理登机手续	bànlǐ dēngjī shǒuxù	check-in
行李	xíngli	baggage
进口	jìnkǒu	entrance
出口	chūkǒu	exit
民航班车	mínháng bānchē	airport bus
请勿吸烟	qǐng wù xīyān	no smoking
紧急出口	jǐnjí chūkǒu	emergency exit
厕所	cèsuǒ	toilet
中国民航	Zhōngguó mínháng	Air China
英国航空公司	Yīngguó hángkōng gōngsī	British Airways
中国银行	Zhōngguó yínháng	Bank of China
护照检查	hùzhào jiǎnchá	passport control

aircraft	fēijī	to arrive	dàodá
flight	hángbān/fēijī	departure tax	jīchǎng fèi
flight number	hángbān hào	where	nǎr
to take off	qǐfēi	airline	hángkōng gōngsī

Information

Does Air China fly to …?	*Zhōngguó mínháng fēi … ma?*
… Xi'an	*… Xī'ān …*
… Kunming	*… Kūnmíng …*
Is there a flight to …?	*Yŏu qù … de fēijī ma?*
… Shanghai	*… Shànghăi …*
… Guilin	*… Guìlín …*
I'd like to fly with Air China	*Wó xiăng chéng Zhōngguó mínháng*
Which airlines fly to …?	*Năge hángkōng gōngsi fēi …?*
How many flights to Xi'an … are there?	*… yóu jǐ tàng fēi Xī'ān de fēijī?*
… a day …	*Měi tiān …*
… a week …	*Měi zhōu …*
What time is … to Guangzhou?	*Qù Guăngzhōu de … jí diăn qǐfēi?*
… the first flight …	*… dì yī bān fēijī …*
… the second flight …	*… dì èr bān fēijī …*
… the next flight …	*… xià yi bān fēijī …*
… the last flight …	*… zuìhòu yi bān fēijī …*
What time does it arrive?	*Jí diăn dàodá?*
Do I have to change planes?	*Wŏ xūyào huàn fēijī ma?*
Where do I change planes?	*Zài năr huàn fēijī?*
Where is the ticket office?	*Shòupiào chù zài năr?*
Where do I pay airport departure tax?	*Zài năr jiāo jīchăng fēi?*
Where is Gate …?	*… dēngjī kŏu zài năr?*
… 11	*Shíyī hào …*
… 23	*Èrshísān hào …*
My luggage is lost	*Wŏde xíngli diū le*
Where is the Air China desk?	*Zhōngguó mínháng chuāngkŏu zài năr?*

Where is the Bank of China?	*Zhōngguó yínháng zài năr?*
Where is the airport bus?	*Mínháng bānchē zài năr?*
Where can I get a taxi?	*Chūzū chē zài năr?*

Tickets

I'd like to buy an airline ticket to …	*Wŏ xiăng măi yī zhāng qù … de fēijī piào*
… Xiamen	*… Xiàmén …*
… Wuhan	*… Wŭhàn …*
One … ticket, please	*Yào yī zhāng …*
… first-class …	*… tóuděng cāng*
… economy-class …	*… jīngjì cāng*
… business-class …	*… shāngwù cāng*
How much is it for …?	*Duō shăo qián …?*
… a single	*… yī zhāng dānchéng piào*
… a return	*… yī zhāng huíchéng piào*
… a child	*… yī zhāng xiăohái piào*
I want to get to Beijing as soon as possible	*Wó xiăng jìnkuài qù Běijīng*
Do you have a seat on the next flight?	*Xià yī hángbān yŏu zuòwèi ma?*
What is my flight number?	*Wŏde hángbān hào shì duō shăo?*
What aircraft is it?	*Shì shénme fēijī?*
What time do I have to check in?	*Jí diăn bànlí dēngjī shŏuxù?*
I'd like to confirm my flight	*Wó xiăng quèrèn wŏde jī piào*
I want to change my reservation	*Wó xiăng găibiàn yùdìng de jī piào*
I want to postpone my return flight	*Wó xiăng tuīchí huíchéng rìqī*
My name is Smith	*Wŏ jiào Smith*
My flight number is …	*Wŏde hángbān hào shì …*

Checking in

I'd like ...	Wǒ yào ...
... a seat by the window	... yī ge kào chuānghu de zuòwèi
... an aisle seat	... yī ge kào zǒuláng de zuòwèi
... a seat next to the emergency exit	... yī ge kào jǐnjí chūkǒu de zuòwèi
Smoking	Xīyān
Non-smoking	Bù xīyān
Which gate is it?	Shì nǎge dēngjī kǒu?
Do I have to collect my luggage when I change planes?	Huàn fēijī shí wǒ yào qǔ xíngli ma?
Can I take this as hand-luggage?	Zhège kéyǐ shǒutí ma?

You may hear

Zhōngguó mínháng bù fēi Guìlín	Air China doesn't fly to Guilin
Yì zhōu sān bān	Three flights a week
Měi tiān yì bān	One flight a day
Shénme shíhou zǒu?	When are you leaving?
Jǐ zhāng piào?	How many tickets?
Tóuděng cāng háishì jīngjì cāng?	First class or economy class?
Nǐde hángbān hào shì BJ líng-yāo-wǔ-sān	Your flight no. is BJ 0153
Bōyīn qī-sì-qī	Boeing 747
Duìbùqǐ, zhège hángbān méi yǒu zuòwèi le	Sorry, there are no seats available on this flight
Nǐ jiāo jīchǎng fèi le ma?	Have you paid the airport departure tax?
Ràng wǒ kànkan shōujù	Show me the receipt, please
Xīyān háishì bù xīyān?	Smoking or non-smoking?
Méi yǒu mínháng bānchē	There is no airport bus
Nǐ kéyǐ zuò chūzūchē	You can take a taxi

Jǐ jiàn xíngli?	How many pieces of luggage?
Nǐde xíngli chāo zhòng le	Your luggage has exceeded the weight limit
Zhège xíngli tài dà, bù kéyi shǒutí	This is too big for hand-luggage
Qǐng chūshì hùzhào	Passport, please

▌ Since very few people in China have private cars and there are only two underground lines in Beijing and as yet no underground in any other city, you can imagine how crowded buses and trams can be, especially during the rush hour.

▌ Buses and trams are numbered according to their route. The Arabic number usually appears above the windscreen and is sometimes printed on the side of the bus or tram. Some bus and tram stops have shelters, but they all have signs with Arabic numbers on them. You can't miss bus and tram stops because there are always people waiting there. The Chinese drive on the right – make sure that you catch the bus or tram going in the correct direction.

▌ One of the methods used to solve the rush hour problem is to divide buses on the same route into fast buses and slow buses. Fast buses stop at a few selected stops, which are sometimes announced when the bus gets to the stop, while slow buses stop at every stop. Trams are not divided in this way as they have shorter routes. The signs for fast and slow buses appear in characters above the windscreen (see **You may see** below). If your destination is the last stop, you have nothing to worry about. If you need to get off somewhere in the middle of that route, however, always ask the bus conductor or other passengers if the bus stops at the place where you want to get off.

▌ When a bus or tram is so full of people that it cannot take any more, the conductor usually asks if there is anybody getting off at the next stop. If nobody wants to get off, it does not stop. Make sure you shout **xià** (Yes, I'll get off) before you get to your stop or tell the conductor where you want to get off as soon as you board.

▌ Buses and trams usually run between 5 a.m. and 11 p.m. The bus conductor can tell you the times of the first and last service. Some buses only run after midnight and they are known as **yèbānchē** (night buses), which will be on the sign at the bus stop (see **You**

may see below). The conductor announces the next stop just before the bus gets there but this announcement will be in Chinese.

■ The driver's job is simply to drive; the fare is collected by a conductor. Fares are very cheap and children under six usually travel free. There are no return tickets or day travel cards but you can buy a monthly pass for use on buses and trams, which always starts from the first day of the month. If you have missed the first week of the month, it's not worth buying the pass. Monthly passes can be bought from ticket offices at main bus stops.

■ You can board a Chinese bus by any door as long as you first make way for passengers getting off. On a very crowded bus, there is no need to be polite; you have to elbow your way through. If there are lots of people blocking the door, always ask if they are getting off at the next stop. If the answer is 'no', you have to work your way through them to the door before it's too late.

■ An alternative to buses and trams are small mini-buses. They are much cheaper than taxis and more comfortable and faster than buses and trams. You can board a mini-bus as long as there's a vacant seat and they stop wherever you like as long as it is not out of their way. However, not every route has a mini-bus service. Ask the locals if there are mini-buses going to your destination. In Beijing, mini-buses are known as **zhāo shǒu tíng** (*lit.* wave hand stop). Mini-buses are much smaller than ordinary buses and they seat 15 to 18 people. You can't stand on a mini-bus as they are very low.

■ Tourist coaches go to popular sightseeing places in major cities (see SIGHTSEEING).

You may see

公共汽车	*gōnggòng qìchē*	bus
公共汽车站	*gōnggòng qìchē zhàn*	bus stop
电车	*diànchē*	tram
小公共汽车	*xiǎo gōnggòng qìchē*	mini-bus

夜班车	*yèbānchē*	night bus
快车	*kuài chē*	fast bus
慢车	*màn chē*	slow bus

You may want to say

Excuse me, where is … bus stop?	*Duìbùqǐ, … chē zhàn zài nǎr?*
… the No. 20 …	*… èrshí lù …*
… the No. 15 …	*… shíwǔ lù …*
Which bus goes to the Beijing Hotel?	*Nǎ lù chē qù Běijīng Fàndiàn?*
How often does this bus run?	*Zhè lù chē duō cháng shíjiān lái yī tàng?*
Have you been waiting long?	*Ní děng le hén jiǔ ma?*
Does this bus stop at …?	*Zhè liàng chē zài … tíng ma?*
… Beijing University	*… Běijīng Dàxué …*
… Yueya Lane	*… Yuèyá hútong …*
What time is your …?	*… jí diǎn?*
… first service	*Tóubān chē …*
… last service	*Mòbān chē …*
Please say it slowly. I didn't understand	*Qǐng màn diǎnr shuō. Wǒ méi tíng dǒng*
Does this bus go to …?	*Zhè shì qù … de chē ma?*
… the railway station	*… huǒchē zhàn …*
… the airport	*… fēijī chǎng …*
… the Art Gallery	*… měishù guǎn …*
Is this …?	*Zhè shì … ma?*
… the No. 10 bus	*… shí lù gōnggòng qìchē …*
… the No. 4 tram	*… sì lù diànchē …*
One ticket to … please	*Yì zhāng qù … de piào*
… Tian'anmen …	*… Tiān'ānmén …*
… the Friendship Store …	*… Yǒuyì Shāngdiàn …*

How much is it?	*Duō shǎo qián?*
Excuse me, what is the next stop?	*Duìbùqǐ, xià yi zhàn shì nǎr?*
Is Wangfujing the next stop?	*Xià yi zhàn shì Wángfújǐng ma?*
Are you getting off at the next stop?	*Nǐ xià yi zhàn xià chē ma?*
Excuse me, I need to get off	*Duìbùqǐ, wǒ yào xià chē*
Yes (in response to 'Anybody getting off?')	*Xià*
Where can I buy a monthly pass?	*Zài nǎr mǎi yuè piào?*
A monthly pass, please	*Wǒ yào yì zhāng yuè piào*

You may hear

Fùjìn méi yǒu èrshí lù chē zhàn	There's no No. 20 bus stop near here
Nǐ kéyi zuò shíwǔ lù gōngòng qìchē	You can take the No. 15 bus
Dàyuē měi shíwǔ fēnzhōng	About every 15 minutes
Shì de, hén jiǔ le	Yes, (I've been waiting) a long time
Bù jiǔ	Not long
Wǒ yǐjing děng le shí fēnzhōng le	I've waited for 10 minutes
Tóubān chē shì zǎoshang liù diǎn	The first bus is at 6 a. m.
Mòbān chē shì wǎnshang shíyī diǎn	The last bus is at 11 p. m.
Yǒu rén mǎi piào ma?	Any fares, please
Nǐ qù nǎr?	Where are you going?
Jǐ zhāng piào?	How many tickets?
Liǎng máo wǔ yì zhāng	Two *mao* and five *fen* per ticket
… yǒu rén xià chē ma?	Anybody getting off at …?
Xià yi zhàn …	… the next stop
Tiān'ānmén …	… Tian'anmen
Xià	Yes (I'm getting off)
Bú xià	No (I'm not getting off)
Tíng	Yes, it stops
Bù tíng	No, it doesn't stop

Xiān zuò shí lù gōnggòng qìchē	Take the No. 10 bus first
Zài dòngwùyuán xià chē	Get off at the zoo
Huàn shíbā lù diànchē	Then change for the No. 18 tram
Nǐ zuò cuò chē le	You've taken the wrong bus
Bié jí	Don't worry
Wǒ dài nǐ qù chē zhàn	I'll take you to the bus stop

Taxis and bicycles

■ There are plenty of taxis in major cities. You can hire them for longer trips as well as short journeys. Taxi fares are based on the type of vehicle and facilities such as air-conditioning, as well as distance. Regardless of what type of taxi you get, there is a flat rate of 10 **yuan** (about 80 pence) which covers the first four kilometres. The cheapest taxi you can get in Beijing is the type which looks like a mini-bus and is painted yellow. It can seat five to six people. You will be charged about one **yuan** per kilometre after the initial 10 **yuan**. Fares for other types of taxi vary from 1.2 **yuan** to two **yuan** per kilometre after the initial 10 **yuan**. Usually, you can see the price at the side window of the car. As not all taxis have a meter and not all of them have the price on them, it's a good idea to agree on the fare with the driver before you get in. It is also a good idea to take a map with you and have your destination written in Chinese characters.

■ There are taxi pick-up points at airports, railway stations, bus stations, tourist hotels and major sightseeing places. You can also stop a taxi if it has the 'For hire' sign on (see **You may see** below) in the street, but do not do this near crossroads as it is against traffic regulations for taxis to stop there.

■ Bicycles can be rented from some tourist hotels and some bicycle-renting shops on a daily basis. You will have to pay a deposit. Every bicycle in China has a number plate – make sure the bicycle you hire has one.

■ Some roads in large cities have cyclists' lanes separated from other traffic, but others don't. The road situation can be very complicated, but motorists do drive fairly slowly.

■ Like car parks, there are bicycle parks in China. Bicycle park attendants, usually retired people, collect a flat fee (usually around two **jiao** per visit) either when you go in or before you leave. You will be given a device with two halves. Lock one half to the bicycle and keep the other half with you. You must hand this device in to the attendant before you can take your bicycle away. Also, always take note of where you leave the bicycle – otherwise you may have difficulty finding yours when it is surrounded by hundreds or thousands of the same kind!

■ There are bicycle repair shops and stands by the road where you can pump up your tyres (or have them pumped up for you), have your bicycle cleaned, and have it fixed if it needs repairing.

You may see

出租车	*chūzūchē*	taxi
空/有空	*kòng/yǒukòng*	for hire
满	*mǎn*	full
出租自行车	*chūzū zìxíngchē*	bicycle for hire

You may want to say

I'd like to get a taxi	*Wó xiǎng jiào chūzūchē*
Could you take me to …?	*Nǐ néng sòng wǒ qù … ma?*
… the Beijing Hotel	*… Běijīng Fàndiàn …*
… the Palace Museum	*… Gù Gōng …*
… this address	*… zhège dìzhǐ …*
… the airport	*… fēijīchǎng …*
How much is it to …?	*Qù … duō shǎo qián?*
… the railway station	*… huǒchē zhàn …*
… the Friendship Store	*… Yǒuyì Shāngdiàn …*
Too expensive	*Tài guì le*
How about 20 *yuan*?	*Èrshí yuán xíng ma?*
Please stop here	*Qǐng tíng chē*
Can you wait for me?	*Nǐ néng děng wǒ ma?*
Twenty minutes	*Èrshí fēnzhōng*

Is that OK?	Xíng ma?
I'll be back soon	Wǒ mǎshàng jiù huílai
Can you come to collect me tonight?	Nǐ jīnwǎn néng lái jiē wǒ ma?
I need to get to the airport by 8 p.m.	Wǒ bā diǎn bìxū gǎn dào fēijīchǎng
You are so kind. Many thanks	Nǐ tài hǎo le. Duō xiè
Keep the change	Bú yòng zhǎo le
Do you have bicycles to rent?	Nǐmen yǒu zìxíngchē chūzū ma?
I'd like to rent a bicycle	Wǒ xiǎng zū ge zìxíngchē
I'd like to cycle to the Summer Palace	Wǒ xiǎng qí zìxíngchē qù Yíhéyuán
Do you know where I can rent a bicycle?	Nǐ zhīdao wǒ kéyǐ zài nǎr zū zìxíngchē ma?
Can I use the pump?	Wǒ kéyǐ yòng yíxià dǎqìtǒng ma?
My bicycle is broken	Wǒde zìxíngchē huài le
Could you fix it?	Nǐ néng xiū ma?
Is it serious?	Yánzhòng ma?
Will it take long?	Xūyào hén jiǔ ma?
How much is it?	Duō shǎo qián?

You may hear

Méi wèntí	No problem
Hǎo de	OK
Nǐ yào qù nǎr?	Where do you want to go?
Dàgài èrshí kuài	About 20 yuan
Yǐjīng yǒu rén dìng le	It has already been booked
Nǐ yǒu dìtú ma?	Have you got a map?
Dǔ chē le	There's a traffic jam
Chē huài le	The car has broken down
Zhè shì dānxíng xiàn	This is one way traffic
Nǐde fàndiàn jiù zài nàr	Your hotel is just over there
Zài zhèr tíng, xíng ma?	Is it OK to stop here?

Yào děng duō jiǔ?	How long do I have to wait?
Duìbùqǐ, wǒ bù néng děng	Sorry, I can't wait
Méi yǒu zìxíngchē	No bicycles
Suóyǒude zìxíngchē dōu zū chūqu le	All the bicycles have been rented out
Míngtiān huì yǒu	We'll have some tomorrow
Qǐng jiāo yì bǎi yuán yājīn	Please pay 100 *yuan* deposit
Zhè shì chē suǒ	Here is the lock to the bicycle
Lúntāi pò le	The tyre has got a puncture
Bù yánzhòng	Not serious
Xiǎo máobìng	It's a small problem

■ There are over 2000 hotels in China and half of them use the star system of international classification. If you are on an organised tour, you will be put into a luxury hotel which is just as good as any Western counterpart. Facilities in these hotels are likely to include an indoor swimming pool, gymnasium, bank, post office, tourist desk, business centre, bar, shops and restaurants. You will find foreign newspapers, English language programmes on satellite television, direct dial telephones and fax machines as well.

■ Luxury hotels are called **fàndiàn**, **jiǔdiàn** or **bīnguǎn** and they are the most expensive. **Lǚguǎn** are mid-range hotels, used essentially by Chinese people, but they do sometimes take foreigners. You may have to share a bathroom there. **Lǚshè** are bottom range inns and are inaccessible to foreigners. If you are a student, it's a good idea to contact those Chinese universities that have **liú xuéshēng gōngyù** (overseas students flats) as they sometimes rent out some flats during vacations (summer vacation is from mid-July to September, and the four weeks' winter vacation is between January and February). These flats are inexpensive and clean, with adequate facilities. Find out the telephone and fax numbers of the universities which rent out flats through the Education Section of the Chinese Embassy (see USEFUL ADDRESSES AND TELEPHONE NUMBERS).

■ As tap water is not always safe to drink, most hotels provide each room with flasks filled with hot boiled water. Don't drink the tap water unless it says it's safe to drink.

■ You'll be asked to show your passport when you check into a hotel and you may be asked to pay a deposit.

■ In some hotels, the rate for a room with double or twin beds is the same regardless of whether there are one or two occupants. Meals are not included as part of the hotel charge. Most luxury hotels accept credit cards, while mid-range and small hotels only accept cash.

■ Further information about Chinese hotels is available from the China International Travel Service (CITS), which has branches in major cities inside China. The National Tourism Administration of People's Republic of China also has overseas offices called 'China National Tourist Office' in the UK, USA, Australia, etc. (see USEFUL ADDRESSES AND TELEPHONE NUMBERS).

You may see

饭店	*fàndiàn*	luxury hotel
酒店	*jiǔdiàn* (in the south)	luxury hotel
宾馆	*bīnguǎn (lit.* guest house*)*	luxury hotel
旅馆	*lǚguǎn*	mid-range hotel
旅社	*lǚshè*	small inn
房价	*fángjià*	charges/rates
单人房间	*dānrén fángjiān*	single room
双人房间	*shuāngrén fángjiān*	double room
卫生间	*wèishēng jiān*	bathroom
餐厅	*cāntīng*	restaurant (in a hotel)
厕所	*cèsuǒ*	toilet
一层	*yī céng*	ground floor
二层	*èr céng*	first floor
服务台	*fúwùtái*	reception
饭店经理	*fàndiàn jīnglǐ*	hotel manager
请勿打扰	*qǐng wù dárǎo*	Please do not disturb
紧急出口	*jǐnjí chūkǒu*	emergency exit
电梯	*diàntī*	lift

Useful words

key	*yàoshi*	vacancy	*kòng fángjiān* (only for hotels)
room	*fángjiān*	to make a reservation	*dìng fángjiān* (only for hotels)
number	*hào*	what time	*jǐ diǎn*
to stay	*dāi/zhù*		

You may want to say

Making a reservation and checking in

I'd like to make a reservation	*Wǒ xiǎng dìng fángjiān*
Are there any vacancies?	*Yǒu kòng fángjiān ma?*
I'd like ...	*Wǒ xiǎng yào ...*
... two single rooms	*... liǎng ge dānrén fángjiān*
... a double room	*... yī ge shuāngrén fángjiān*
How much is it ...?	*Duō shǎo qián ...?*
... per room	*... yī jiān*
... per person	*... yī ge rén*
Do you have anything cheaper?	*Yǒu piányi yìxiē de ma?*
Can I pay by credit card?	*Wǒ kéyǐ yòng xìnyòng kǎ fù zhàng ma?*
From ... for four nights	*Cóng ... kāshǐ zhù sì tiān*
... 1 July ...	*... qīyuè yī hào ...*
... 26 May ...	*... wǔyuè èrshíliù hào ...*
I'd like a ...	*Wǒ xiǎng yào yī ge ...*
... quiet room	*... ānjìng de fángjiān*
... ground floor room	*... zài yī céng de fángjiān*
I made a reservation for a double room	*Wǒ dìng le yī ge shuāngrén fángjiān*
My name is ...	*Wǒ jiào ...*

I reserved it for four nights	*Wǒ dìng le sì tiān*
Now I only need it for three nights	*Xiànzài, wó zhǐ xūyào zhù sān tiān*
Please cancel one night	*Qǐng qùdiào yī tiān*

Information

Is there ... in the room?	*Fángjiān lǐ yǒu ... ma?*
... a telephone ...	*... diànhuà ...*
... air-conditioning ...	*... kōng tiáo ...*
... a television ...	*... diànshì ...*
Is there a shower in the bathroom?	*Wèishēngjiān lǐ yǒu línyù ma?*
Is there ... in the hotel?	*Fàndiàn lǐ yǒu ... ma?*
... a bank ...	*... yínháng ...*
... a swimming pool ...	*... yóuyǒng chí ...*
... a gymnasium ...	*... jiànshēnfáng ...*
... a restaurant ...	*... cāntīng ...*
... a bar ...	*... jiǔbā ...*
What time is ...?	*Jǐ diǎn chī ...?*
... breakfast	*... zǎofàn*
... dinner	*... wǎnfàn*
Do you serve a Western-style breakfast?	*Nǐmen gōngyìng xī shì zǎocān ma?*
What time does the bar open?	*Jiǔbā jǐ diǎn kāimén?*
Do you have an English newspaper?	*Nǐmen yǒu Yīngwén bàozhǐ ma?*
Excuse me, where is the lift?	*Duìbùqǐ, diàntī zài nǎr?*
What time must I check out?	*Wǒ bìxū jǐ diǎn bànlǐ líkāi shǒuxù?*

Problems

The ... in my room is not working	*Wǒ fángjiān lǐ de ... huài le*
... telephone ...	*... diànhuà ...*
... TV ...	*... diànshì ...*
... light ...	*... diàndēng ...*

73

The shower is broken	*Línyù huài le*
There are no bath towels	*Méi yǒu yùjīn*
My room is a bit cold	*Wǒde fángjiān yǒu diánr lěng*
My room is too hot	*Wǒde fángjiān tài rè le*
My neighbour is very noisy	*Wǒde gébì hén chǎo*
I've lost the key to my room	*Wǒ diū le fángjiān de yàoshi*
I'd like to see the duty manager	*Wó xiǎng jiàn zhíbān jīnglǐ*
Can I have another ...?	*Kéyi zài géi wǒ yī ge ... ma?*
... blanket	*... tǎnzi ...*
... pillow	*... zhěntóu ...*
... bath towel	*... yùjīn ...*

You may hear

Duìbùqǐ, méi yǒu kòng fángjiān	Sorry, we have no vacancies
Nǐ yào dān jiān háishì shuāng jiān?	Do you want a single room or a double room?
Yí ge rén háishì liǎng ge rén?	For one or two people?
Kǒngpà méi yǒu zài piányi de le	We haven't got anything cheaper, I'm afraid
Zhè shì zuì piányi de	This is the cheapest
Nǐ zhù jǐ tiān?	How many nights are you staying?
Bù shōu xìnyòng kǎ	We don't accept credit cards
Zhǐ shōu xiànjīn	We only accept cash
Duìbùqǐ, méi yǒu xī shì zǎocān	Sorry, we don't serve a Western-style breakfast
Zǎofàn cóng qī diǎn bàn dào bā diǎn bàn	Breakfast is from 7.30 to 8.30 a.m.
Wǎnfàn cóng liù diǎn dào jiǔ diǎn	Dinner is from 6 to 9 p.m.
Wǒ huì chǔlǐ de	I'll see to it
Zhēn bàoqiàn	Many apologies

Telephones

■ Making local calls is very easy and costs very little. Telephone numbers in large cities usually consist of seven or eight digits. In some small cities, you will find six or even five digits in a telephone number. The dialling tone, ringing tone and engaged tone are similar to that of Western telephone systems.

■ You can dial direct between the main cities in China with little difficulty. All the area codes in China begin with an (0). For example, (010) for Beijing, (021) for Shanghai, (029) for Xi'an and (020) for Guangzhou. National calls are slightly more expensive than local calls. All national calls cost 50 percent less between 9 p.m. and 6 a.m.

■ Public phones which allow you to dial international numbers direct can only be found in large cities. Watch out for the sign IDD (international direct dialling), which is in Roman letters. You can also make international calls from most luxury hotels but you may have to pay a surcharge.

■ Making international phone calls from China is expensive and there is no cheap rate. To make international calls from China, dial (00) first, followed by the country code. For example, the country code for the UK is (44), followed by the area code without (0). If you want to call a London number with an 0171 code from China, dial: 00-44-171 plus the number. The country code for the USA is (1) so if you want to call a Los Angeles number with the area code (213) from China, dial: 00-1-213 followed by the number. The country code for China is (86). To call a number in China, for example 010-63678561, dial the international code from your country, followed by: 86-10-63678561.

■ Public telephone facilities in China are still rather backward. Coin phones and card phones are relatively new and they don't always work. Also, the phone cards which you use in one city cannot be used in another city. In Beijing, there are many public phone booths which are attended by assistants. You first tell the assistant where you wish to call and you will be asked to put down a deposit (which, of course, will be refunded if the connection cannot be made). After the call, you will be handed a computer printout and asked to pay the balance. It is a good idea to time your call in case the computer printout is incorrect. Some public telephones are in small shops and others are actually located inside family homes, so don't be surprised if the public telephone sign leads you to a private house.

▌ Alternatively, you can go to the local **yóu diàn jú** (Postal & Telecommunications Office) or **diànbào diànhuà** (Telegrams & Telephones) to make your calls. You can make calls in some **yóu jú** (Post Offices) as well.

▌ If you want to send a fax, you need to go to a large modern hotel where such services are usually provided. However this can be very expensive.

▌ On the phone, **wèi** (hello) is sometimes used instead of **ní hǎo** (hello); it is a little less formal. Never use **wèi** in face-to-face communication.

▌ To read telephone numbers, simply say each digit individually (see NUMBERS). When saying telephone numbers, **yāo** (one) is used instead of **yī** (one) as **yī** and **qī** (seven) may cause confusion. For example, the telephone number 467217 is read **sì-liù-qī-èr-yāo-qī**.

▌ (See USEFUL ADDRESSES AND TELEPHONE NUMBERS for telephone enquiries)

You may see

公用电话	gōngyòng diànhuà	public phone
电话亭	diànhuà tíng	telephone booth
邮电局	yóu diàn jú	Post and Telecommunications Office
邮局	yóu jú	Post Office
电报电话	diànbào diànhuà	Telegrams and Telephones
国内直拨	guónèi zhí bō	national direct dialling
国际直拨	guójì zhí bō	international direct dialling

Useful words

telephone	*diànhuà (lit. electrical talk)*
to make phone calls	*dǎ diànhuà*
engaged	*zhànxiàn*
didn't get through	*dǎ bù tōng*
... does/did not work	*huài le*
long-distance call	*chángtú diànhuà*
area code	*dìqū hào*
telephone number	*diànhuà hàomǎ*
hello	*wèi*

You may want to say

Information

Is there a telephone ...?	*... yǒu diànhuà ma?*
... nearby	*Fùjìn ...*
... in this restaraunt	*Zhège fàndiàn lí ...*
... on this floor	*Zhè céng lóu shang ...*
... in my room	*Wǒde fángjiān lí ...*
Where is ...?	*... zài nǎr?*
... a public telephone	*Gōngyòng diànhuà ...*
... an international direct dial telephone	*Guójì zhíbō diànhuà ...*
... the post office where I can make phone calls	*Kéyǐ dǎ diànhuà de yóu jú ...*
... a coin phone	*Tóubì diànhuà ...*
A telephone card ... please	*Yào ... de diànhuà kǎ*
... for 100 *yuan* ...	*... yì zhāng yì bǎi yuán ...*
... for 50 *yuan* ...	*... yì zhāng wǔshí yuán ...*

I'd like to make … please	*Wǒ xiǎng dǎ …*
… an international call …	*… yī ge guójì diànhuà*
… a call to Shanghai …	*… yī ge Shànghǎi de diànhuà*
… a reverse-charge call …	*… yī ge duìfāng fùkuǎn diànhuà*
What's the area code for …?	*… de dìqū hào shì duō shǎo?*
… Guangzhou	*Guǎngzhōu …*
… Fujian	*Fújiàn …*
What's the country code for America?	*Měiguó de guójiā hào shì duō shǎo?*
Can I make an international call here?	*Zhèr kěyi dǎ guójì diànhuà ma?*
Can I use your phone?	*Wǒ kěyi yòng yíxià nǐde diànhuà ma?*
Can I dial London direct on this phone?	*Zhège diànhuà kěyi zhíbō Lúndūn ma?*
What's the charge for calling …?	*… duō shǎo qián?*
… the UK	*Dǎ Yīngguó …*
… Canada	*Dǎ Jiānádà …*
I only spoke for two minutes	*Wǒ zhí dǎ le liǎng fēnzhōng*
What's wrong? We were cut off in the middle	*Zěnme huíshì? Dǎ le yī bàn jiù qiē duàn le*
It's a bad line	*Xiànlù bù qīngchu*
Could you try again?	*Qǐng zài shìshi*
I'd like to call …	*Wǒ xiǎng gěi … dǎ diànhuà*
… Professor Mu	*… Mù jiàoshòu …*
… our interpreter	*… wǒménde fānyì …*
Do you have his/her telephone number?	*Nǐ yǒu tāde diànhuà hàomǎ ma?*

On the phone

Hello, it's Mary	*Wèi, wǒ shì Mary*
Is Mr. Xu Hong in?	*Xǔ Hóng xiānsheng zài ma?*
Extension 266, please	*Qǐng jiē èr-liù-liù fēnjī*

Miss Lin in Foreign Affairs, please	*Qǐng jiē Wàishì Chù de Lín xiǎojie*
When will he/she be back?	*Tā shénme shíhou huílai?*
When will he/she finish the meeting?	*Tā shénme shíhou kāi wán huì?*
May I leave a message?	*Wǒ kéyi liú ge huà ma?*
Please tell him/her I called. My name is Mary Collin	*Qǐng gàosu tā wǒ dǎ le diànhuà. Wǒ jiào Mary Collin*
I'm in China now. My telephone number is 022 881091	*Wǒ xiànzài zài Zhōngguó. Wǒde diànhuà hàomǎ shì líng-èr-èr, bā-bā-yāo-líng-jiǔ-yāo*
Please ask him/her to call me	*Qǐng ràng tā gěi wó dǎ diànhuà*
I'll call back later	*Wǒ yìhuǐr zài dǎ*
Sorry, I didn't hear it	*Duìbùqǐ, wǒ méi tīng qīng*
Could you repeat it, please?	*Qǐng zài shuō yī biàn*
Sorry, I've dialled the wrong number	*Duìbùqǐ, wó dǎ cuò le*
I have an enquiry	*Wó xiǎng wèn yī jiàn shì*
Telephone number for the Beijing Hotel, please	*Qǐng gěi wǒ Běijīng Fàndiàn de hàomǎ*

You may hear

Duìbùqǐ, zhèr bù néng dǎ guójì diànhuà	Sorry, you can't make international calls here
Zhège diànhuà huài le	This phone is broken
Nǐ yào dǎ de diànhuà hàomǎ shì duōshǎo?	What's the number you want to call?
Méi rén jiē diànhuà	There is no answer
Qǐng jiāo yī bǎi kuài yājīn	One hundred *yuan* deposit, please
Dǎ Yīngguó měi fēnzhōng èrshíbā kuài	Twenty-eight *yuan* per minute to call the UK
Ní hǎo. Běijīng Fàndiàn	Hello, Beijing Hotel
Duìbùqǐ, zhànxiàn	Sorry, it's engaged
Nín yìhuǐr dǎ lái, hǎo ma?	Can you call back later?

Zhèr méi rén jiào Wáng Lín	There's no one called Wang Lin here
Wáng xiǎojie …	Miss Wang …
… bú zài	… is not in
… chī zhōngfàn qù le	… has gone for lunch
… kāihuì qù le	… has gone to a meeting
Qǐng wèn, nín shì nǎ yī wèi?	Who is speaking, please?
Wèi, ní zhǎo shéi?	Hello, who do you wish to speak to?
Ní xiǎng liú huà ma?	Would you like to leave a message?
Qíng dĕng yíxià	Could you hold, please?
Wǒ xiànzài hěn máng, nǐ guò shí fēnzhōng dǎ lái, xíng ma?	I'm very busy right now. Can you call back in 10 minutes?
Jiànmiàn hòu zài xì tán	We'll have a good talk about it when we meet

Posting letters and postcards

▌ Letter boxes in China are green in colour and post offices have their signs against a green background. In most post offices, you can also make phone calls and send telegrams.

▌ Post offices are open from 8.30 a.m. until 5.30 p.m. In large cities, there is usually a main post office which provides all services and is open 24 hours a day, seven days a week. All post offices open on public holidays. Some close one day during the week.

▌ If you simply want to send a letter or postcard, you can buy stamps at the reception in your hotel and hand in the letter or postcard to the receptionist. Some tourist hotels have a post office inside. If you want to send a parcel, you will have to go to a post office. If you send a parcel to an address inside China, it is advisable to have the address written in Chinese characters and hand it over to a member of post office staff, who will help you fill in a form. If it's international, the form will be in English. Post offices in small towns have little experience of dealing with international matters, so save your parcels until you are in a large city.

▌ Different services at a post office are dealt with at different counters. For example, you buy stamps at one counter and send parcels at another. Make sure you are at the right counter before joining the queue.

▌ To send a letter to another city inside China, you can send it by ordinary mail, air mail or fast delivery. It's a good idea to have the address written down in Chinese characters and ask a Chinese person to copy it onto the envelope for you. This will prevent the letter being delayed.

You may see

邮局	yóu jú	post office
邮电局	yóudiàn jú	postal and telephone office
信筒	xìn tǒng	letter box
国际邮政	guójì yóuzhèng	international postal service
包裹	bāoguǒ	parcels
邮票	yóupiào	stamps
航空	hángkōng	air mail
电报	diànbào	telegram
国际电话	guójì diànhuà	international telephone

Useful words

recorded delivery	guàhào		postcode	yóubiān
fast delivery	kuài dì		address	dìzhǐ
envelope	xìnfēng		ordinary mail	píng xìn
postcard	míngxìnpiàn			

You may want to say

Is there a post office in the hotel?	Fàndiàn lí yǒu yóu jú ma?
I'd like to send a …	Wó xiǎng jì …
… letter	… xìn
… postcard	… míngxìnpiàn
Do you sell stamps?	Ní yǒu yóupiào ma?
Can I post these postcards here?	Zhèr kéyi jì míngxìnpiàn ma?
Where is the letter box?	Xìn tǒng zài nǎr?
Where is the post office?	Yóu jú zài nǎr?
Is there a post office nearby?	Fùjìn yǒu yóu jú ma?

I'd like to send it by …	*Wǒ xiǎng jì …*
… air mail	*… hángkōng*
… recorded delivery	*… guàhào*
… fast delivery	*… kuài dì*
How much is it to send a letter to …?	*Jì yì fēng qù … de xìn duō shǎo qián?*
… America	*… Měiguó*
… Shanghai	*… Shànghǎi*
How much is it to send a postcard to …?	*Jì yì zhāng dào … de míngxìnpiàn duō shǎo qián?*
… the UK	*… Yīngguó*
… Hong Kong	*… Xiānggǎng*
Two stamps for postcards to the UK, please	*Liǎng zhāng jì Yīngguó de míngxìnpiàn de yóupiào*
I'd like to send a parcel to America	*Wǒ xiǎng jì yí ge bāoguǒ dào Měiguó*
There is/are … inside	*Lǐmian shì …*
… a book …	*… yì běn shū*
… some gifts …	*… yìxiē lǐwù*
How long does it take?	*Jǐ tiān néng dào?*
It's urgent	*Zhè hěn jí*
Could you copy this address for me, please?	*Nǐ kéyi bāng wǒ chāo yíxià dìzhǐ ma?*
Do you have any commemorative stamps?	*Yǒu jìniàn yóupiào ma?*

You may hear

Yǒu yóu jú	Yes, there is a post office
Wǒ dài nǐ qù	I'll take you there
Duìbùqǐ, zhèr méi yǒu jú	Sorry, there is no post office here
Wǒ zhèr yǒu yóupiào	I've got stamps here
Nǐ xiǎng jì shénme?	What would you like to post?

Wǒ kéyi tì nǐ jì xìn hé míngxìnpiàn	I can post letters and postcards for you
Fàndiàn hòumian yǒu ge yóu jú	There's a post office behind the hotel
Jì píng xìn háishi hángkōng?	Ordinary mail or air mail?
Bāoguó lǐmian shì shénme?	What's in the parcel?
Chāo zhòng le	It has exceeded the weight limit
Hái yào fù liǎng kuài qián	You need to pay another two *yuan*
Qǐng tián zhè zhāng dānzi	Please fill in this form

Eating and drinking

■ Chinese people place a lot of importance on eating. Chinese cuisine is without doubt among the finest in the world with its emphasis on freshness, taste, presentation and surprising variety. There are regional differences in Chinese cuisine and you will also find different dishes in various parts of the country. For example, Sichuan food is famous for its use of chilli and pepper, while Cantonese food emphasises freshness, with rather mild flavours. Different places usually offer their own specialities; for example, one of Beijing's specialities is Beijing roast duck.

■ While some restaurants offer a wide range of dishes, others specialise in noodles or dumplings. Restaurants which are attached to large hotels are expensive and offer good quality Chinese food, and they are likely to have knives and forks as well as chopsticks. If you can't manage chopsticks, it's a good idea to bring your own knife and fork as most restaurants only have chopsticks and spoons. Most large restaurants make it obvious whether they do Cantonese cooking, Sichuan cooking or any other types of cooking by giving themselves proper names such as 'Sichuan Flavour Restaurant' (see **You may see** below). You can find Western food in some large hotels.

■ If you are concerned about your budget, try small restaurants. Many small restaurants are family-run and offer authentic Chinese food, friendly service and good value for money. It's always a good idea to ask the locals to recommend their favourite eating places. In some cities, there are **yè shì** (evening markets) where you can find food stalls in the street. It's an interesting experience as you can watch how each dish is cooked. If you are worried about hygiene, bring your own bowl and chopsticks.

■ Most Chinese restaurants are noisy and crowded. A busy restaurant is always a sign of good cooking. When Chinese people eat out, they like to have fun. During such occasions, it seems to foreigners that they are fighting and quarrelling, but in actual fact they are just encouraging each other to drink or eat more. Table manners are not an issue. You can do whatever you like – make noises while eating noodles or drinking the soup, hold the bowl close to your mouth, etc.

▌ Chinese menus in some of the larger restaurants are very difficult to understand as they give few clues as to the ingredients of each dish. In many cases, dishes are named according to their appearance rather than contents. For example, visitors will be relieved to know that a dish called 'Ants Climbing the Tree' is actually a stir-fried dish with minced meat and some bean noodles. Don't be scared by the menu! Always ask what the dishes are (see **Menu reader** below).

▌ A typical Chinese meal consists of plain boiled rice (in the south) or steamed buns/plain noodles (in the north) accompanied by several dishes and probably one soup, and they are shared among everyone at the table. Usually, all dishes are served and eaten at the same time. When alcoholic drinks are ordered, it is customary to start with some cold dishes followed by hot dishes (in terms of temperature). Most Chinese people don't have a dessert after their meal but larger restaurants may serve pieces of melon or other fruit to mark the end of a meal. However, you don't have to follow any of the above rules. You can simply order what you like in most restaurants. If you are on your own, for example, you can have a soup with some steam buns or one hot dish with some rice, if that's what you want. If you fancy some cold dishes, you can have them without alcoholic drinks; or order alcoholic drinks with hot dishes.

▌ Most Chinese restaurants only accept cash payment. Only those which are attached to large hotels accept credit cards.

▌ If you eat out with friends, turn up on time or a bit earlier. If you are invited to a Chinese person's house for a meal, it's better to turn up 10 to 15 minutes earlier than the agreed time. This is because it's polite to offer help in the kitchen, and the host or hostess won't start stir-frying until guests arrive as Chinese dishes taste best when they are fresh from the wok.

▌ When your hosts apologise for the bad cooking or for not having made enough dishes when in fact 10 dishes are on the table, you should disagree by saying the food is delicious and there are more than enough dishes. Don't take their comments as real apologies.

▌ During the meal, the host or hostess will automatically put food into your plate or bowl and refill your glass as soon as it is empty; otherwise they feel they are not looking after their guests properly. It is accepted etiquette for people to reach across the dining table for food, soya sauce, salt, pepper, etc. Certainly, if the object is beyond the reach, they will ask someone at the table to pass it.

▌ Chinese breakfast is often the most difficult meal for foreigners. A typical breakfast consists of rice porridge, steamed bread with preserved vegetables or salted eggs. Soya milk and deep-fried sticks of bread are also very popular. If none of these appeals to you, go to a large hotel's restaurant or café where Western-style breakfast is served, or bring your own coffee with you.

▌ **Jiǔ** refers to all types of alcoholic drink, including spirits, wine and beer. Chinese people like sweet wine rather than dry, and red wine is more popular than white. Most Chinese people only drink when they eat. Bars are a fairly new phenomenon due to influence from the West.

▌ When you offer something, be it drink, food or help, to Chinese people, make sure you make your offer two or three times as it is part of Chinese culture to refuse the offer initially out of politeness.

▌ The Chinese equivalent of 'Yes, please' in response to an offer is 'Want, thank you' as the word 'please' (**qǐng**) is never used for this purpose.

You may see

餐馆/饭馆	cānguǎn/fànguǎn	restaurant
快餐店	kuài cāndiàn	fast food
咖啡厅	kāfēi tīng	café
茶馆	chá guǎn	tea house
酒吧	jiǔbā	bar
川菜	Chuān cài	Sichuan cuisine

粤菜	Yuè cài	Cantonese cuisine
菜单	càidān	menu
大盘	dà pán	large dish
中盘	zhōng pán	medium
小盘	xiǎo pán	small dish
米饭	mǐfàn	rice
面/面条	miàn/miàntiáo	noodles
饺子	jiǎozi	Chinese dumplings (with meat and vegetable fillings)
春卷	chūnjuǎn	spring rolls
包子	bāozi	steamed buns with various fillings
汤	tāng	soup
鸡	jī	chicken
猪肉	zhūròu	pork
牛肉	niúròu	beef
羊肉	yángròu	lamb
海鲜	hǎixiān	seafood
鸭	yā	duck
豆腐	dòufu	tofu/bean curd
蔬菜	shūcài	vegetables

Useful words

Chinese food	Zhōng cān	chopsticks	kuàizi
Western food	Xī cān	spoon	sháozi
breakfast	zǎofàn	fork	chāzi
lunch	wǔfàn / zhōngfàn	knife	dāo
dinner	wǎnfàn	bowl	wǎn
vegetarian food	sù cài / sù shí	plate	pánzi

Ingredients and tastes

Please pass me the ...	*Qǐng dì gěi wǒ ...*
... salt	*... yán*
... soy sauce	*... jiàngyóu*
... vinegar	*... cù*
Could I have some ...?	*Wǒ kéyǐ yào yìxiē ... ma?*
... sesame oil	*... xiāng yóu*
... pepper	*... hújiāo*
... sugar	*... táng*
This dish is too ...	*Zhège cài tài ... le*
... salty	*... xián*
... sweet	*... tián*
... sour	*... suān*
... hot (temperature)	*... tàng*
This dish is a little bit ...	*Zhège cài yǒu yìdiǎnr ...*
... under-salted	*... dàn*
... cold	*... liáng*
... hot (chilli hot)	*... là*
Please don't put in any ...	*Qǐng bú yào fàng ...*
... chilli	*... làjiāo/làzi*
... Chinese Sichuan pepper	*... huājiāo*
... monosodium glutamate	*... wèijīng*
... ginger	*... shēngjiāng*
... garlic	*... dàsuàn*
Is it a ... dish?	*Zhège shì ... cài ma?*
... hot (temperature) ...	*... rè ...*
... cold ...	*... liáng ...*

| ... spicy ... | ... là ... |
| What's in the filling? | Shì shénme xiànr? |

Ordering some typical dishes

I'd like to have one portion of ...	Wǒ xiǎng yào yī fèn ...
... Chinese dumplings	... jiǎozi
... spring rolls	... chūnjuǎn
... steamed buns with various fillings	... bāozi
... noodles	... miàn/miàntiáo
... rice	... mǐfàn
... egg-fried rice	... dàn chǎo fàn
... fried noodles	... chǎo miàn
I'd like to have two ...	Wǒ xiǎng yào liǎng ge ...
... steam buns/bread	... mántou
... pancakes	... bǐng
... wonton soups	... húntun tāng
... seafood soups	... hǎixiān tāng
... hot and sour soups	... suānlà tāng
I'll have a small plate of ... please	Wǒ yào yī xiǎo pán ...
... sautéed king prawns ...	... yóumèn dà xiā
... braised fish in soy sauce ...	... hóng shāo yú
... stir-fried mixed vegetables ...	... chǎo shícài
... sweet and sour pork ...	... gúlǎo ròu/tángcù ròu
I like ...	Wǒ xǐhuan ...
... roast duck	... kǎo yā
... Mongolian hot pot	... shuàn yángròu
... crispy deep-fried chicken	... xiāngsū jī
... hot pot	... huǒ guō
... tofu in Sichuan sauce	... málà dòufu

Ordering drinks

I'll have a … please	*Wǒ yào yī ge …*
… beer …	*… píjiǔ*
… coconut drink …	*… yēzi zhī*
… orange juice …	*… júzi zhī*
… cola …	*… kělè*
We'd like to have a bottle of …	*Wǒmen xiǎng yào yī píng …*
… white wine	*… bái pútaojiǔ*
… dry white wine	*… gān bái pútaojiǔ*
… red wine	*… hóng pútaojiǔ*
… rice wine	*… mǐ jiǔ*
Could I have some … please?	*Wǒ kéyi yào yìxiē … ma?*
… Chinese tea …	*… Zhōngguó chá …*
… black coffee …	*… hēi kāfēi …*
… coffee with milk …	*… kāfēi jiā niúnǎi*
… cold milk …	*… liáng niúnǎi*
… mineral water …	*… kuàngquán shuǐ …*
… water with ice …	*… shuǐ jiā bīngkuài …*
Another…, please	*Zài yào …*
… bottle of beer …	*… yī píng píjiǔ*
… glass of wine …	*… yī bēi pútaojiǔ*
… pot of tea …	*… yī hú chá*

Getting things in a food stall/fast food shop/café

What's this?	*Zhè shì shénme?*
I'll have two of these, please	*Wǒ yào liǎng ge zhè zhǒng de*
I'd like to have … please	*Wǒ xiǎng yào …*
… a box of food …	*… yī ge hé fàn*
… a bowl of noodles in soup …	*… yī wǎn tāng miàn*

... 10 dumplings ...	... shí ge jiǎozi
... four steamed dumplings ...	... sì ge bāozi
... two sticks of barbecued mutton ...	... liǎng ge kǎo yángròu chuàn
... a coffee with two pieces of toast ...	... yī ge kāfēi, liǎng piàn kǎo miànbāo
... a cup of hot milk with one piece of cake ...	... yī bēi rè niúnǎi, yī kuài dàngào
No sugar in my coffee	Kāfēi lǐ bú yào táng
Coffee with a drop of milk, please	Kāfēi lǐ jiā yìdiǎnr niúnǎi
Is it pork or beef?	Zhè shì zhūròu háishi niúròu?
How much is it?	Duō shǎo qián?
I'll take it away	Wǒ ná zǒu chī
Can you put it in a bag, please?	Qǐng fàng zài yī ge dàizi li, hǎo ma?

Booking a table

Is there a good restaurant near here?	Fùjìn yóu hǎo cānguǎn ma?
What time does it open?	Jǐ diǎn kāimén?
I'd like to book a table for ...	Wǒ xiǎng dìng yī zhāng ... zhuō
... two	... liǎng rén ...
... four	... sì rén ...
It's for ... at ...	Shì ...
... tonight ... 7 p.m.	... jīntiān wǎnshang qī diǎn
... tomorrow night ... 8.30 p.m.	... míngtiān wǎnshang bā diǎn bàn
My name is Smith	Wǒ xìng Smith

At the restaurant

A table for two, please	Yào liǎng rén zhuō
My name is Smith, and I have a table booked for four people	Wǒ xìng Smith, wǒ dìng le yī ge zhuōzi, sì ge rén
Could I have a menu, please?	Wǒ kéyǐ kàn yíxià càidān ma?

You do the ordering, please	*Ní diǎn ba*
I don't know what to order	*Wǒ bù zhīdao diǎn shénme*
Can you recommend a dish or two?	*Ní kéyi géi wǒmen tuījiàn yì liǎng ge cài ma?*
Do you have dim-sum dishes?	*Nǐmen yǒu Guǎngdōng diǎnxīn ma?*
How much is this dish?	*Zhège cài duō shǎo qián?*
Do you have knives and forks?	*Ní yǒu dāo hé chāzi ma?*
What's the typical local dish?	*Shénme shì dāngdì fēngwèi cài?*
We'll go for the set menu	*Wǒmen chī tào cài*
I like spicy food	*Wó xǐhuan chī làde*
I'm a vegetarian	*Wǒ chī sù*
I don't drink (alcohol)	*Wǒ bù hē jiǔ*
I can't eat ...	*Wǒ bù néng chī ...*
... meat	*... ròu*
... beef	*... niúròu*
... egg	*... jī dàn*
... mushrooms	*... mógu*
... onion	*... yángcōng*
... seafood	*... hǎixiān*
... prawns	*... xiā*
Where's the toilet, please?	*Qǐng wèn, cèsuǒ/xíshǒujiān zài nǎr?*
Could I smoke here?	*Wǒ kéyi zài zhèr chōuyān ma?*
May I have the bill, please?	*Qǐng jié zhàng ba*
Where do I pay?	*Zài nǎr fù qián?*
Can I pay by credit card?	*Kéyi yòng xìnyòng kǎ fù zhàng ma?*

At the dinner table

Cheers!	*Gānbēi* (lit. empty one's glass)!
Your good health	*Zhù nǐ shēntǐ jiànkāng*
I can't use chopsticks	*Wǒ bú huì yòng kuàizi*

More … please	*Wǒ zài yào yìxiē …*
… pancakes …	*… bǐng*
… rice …	*..mǐfán*
… tea …	*… chá*
This dish is delicious	*Zhège cài hén hǎochī*
This fish is very fresh	*Zhè tiáo yú hěn xiān*
Your food is very good	*Nǐde cài zuò de zhēn hǎo*
Would you like some more?	*Nǐ hái yào ma?*
Yes, please	*Yào, xièxie*
A little more, please	*Yào yìdiǎnr, xièxie*
No more, thanks	*Wǒ bú yào le, xièxie*
I am full	*Wǒ chī bǎo le*

You may hear

Qǐng wèn, jǐ wèi?	How many of you, please?
Qǐng gēn wǒ lái	Please follow me
Diǎn cài ma, xiānsheng?	Ready to order, sir?
Nín xiǎng chī shénme, xiǎojie?	What would you like to have, miss?
Nín xiǎng hē shénme?	What would you like to drink?
Nín yào dāo chā ma?	Would you like a knife and fork?
Shì zhūròu xiànr	It's pork filling
Nǐ chī guo jiǎozi ma?	Have you had dumplings?
Nǐ hē guo Qīngdǎo píjiǔ ma?	Have you had Qingdao beer?
Qīngdǎo píjiǔ méi yǒu le	We are running out of Qingdao beer
Běijīng píjiǔ xíng ma?	How about Beijing beer?
Qǐng màn man yòng (formal)	Enjoy your meal
Qǐng chī (food)/*Qǐng hē* (drinks)	Help yourself
Suíbiàn chī (said by host to guest)	Help yourself to whatever (dish) you like
Duō chī yìxiē	Have some more

Hǎo chī ma?	Is everything all right? (food only)	
Hái yào biéde ma?	Would you like to have anything else?	
Yòng wán le ma (formal)*?/*		
Chī wán le ma (informal)*?*	Have you finished?	
Zhè shì nǐde zhàngdān	Here's your bill	
Zhè shì zhǎo nǐde língqián	Here's your change	
Xièxie guānglín (formal)	Thank you for coming	
Huānyíng zài lái	Come again, please	

Menu reader

This is by no means an exhaustive list of dishes. Only the basic food items and some most often encountered dishes and cooking methods are given below. Any food that is grain-based is classified as **zhǔshí** (*lit.* main food) or **fàn** (food) and meat, fish, vegetables, etc. are classified as **cài** (*lit.* vegetables).

Rice-based food

boiled rice	*bái mǐfàn*	白米饭
egg stir-fried rice	*dàn chǎo fàn*	蛋炒饭
Yangzhou stir-fried rice	*Yángzhōu chǎo fàn*	扬州炒饭
glutinous rice wrapped in bamboo leaves (with meat or sweet flavoured ingredients)	*zòngzi*	棕子
rice porridge	*dàmǐ xīfàn*	大米稀饭
crispy rice topped with seafood, meat or vegetables	*guōbā fàn*	锅巴饭
stir-fried rice cake	*chǎo nián gāo*	炒年糕

Wheat-based food

steamed buns	*mántou*	馒头
steamed twisted rolls	*huājuǎn*	花卷
pancake	*bǐng*	饼
pancake with sesame seeds	*shāo bǐng*	烧饼
pancake with spring onion	*cōng yóu bǐng*	葱油饼
pancake with fillings	*xiànr bǐng*	馅饼
steamed dumplings with fillings	*bāozi*	包子
… with pork	*zhūròu bāozi*	猪肉包子
… with barbecued pork	*chā shāo bāozi*	叉烧包子
… with beef	*niúròu bāozi*	牛肉包子
… with lamb	*yángròu bāozi*	羊肉包子
… with 'three fresh' (with three ingredients, usually meat with seafood)	*sānxiān bāozi*	三鲜包子
… with vegetables	*sù bāozi*	素包子
… with red-bean paste	*dòushā bāozi*	豆沙包子
small steamed dumplings with fillings	*xiǎolóng bāozi*	小笼包子
noodles	*miàn / miàntiáo*	面/面条
fried noodles with shredded pork	*zhūròu sī chǎo miàn*	猪肉丝炒面
fried noodles with bean-sprouts	*dòuyá chǎo miàn*	豆芽炒面
noodles with minced meat and soy bean sauce	*zhá jiàng miàn*	炸酱面
noodles with beef	*niúròu miàn*	牛肉面
noodles in soup	*tāng miàn*	汤面
dumplings	*jiǎozi*	饺子
fried dumplings (pot stickers)	*guōtiē*	锅贴
steamed dumplings	*zhēng jiǎozi*	蒸饺子

dumplings with vegetable fillings	*sù jiǎozi*	素饺子
won ton	*húntun*	馄饨
spring rolls	*chūn juǎn*	春卷

Breakfast

Chinese-style

steamed buns	*mántou*	馒头
steamed twisted rolls	*huājuǎn*	花卷
small steamed dumplings with fillings	*xiǎolóng bāozi*	小笼包子
soy milk	*dòu jiāng*	豆浆
deep-fried dough sticks	*yóutiáo*	油条
rice porridge	*dàmǐ xīfàn*	大米稀饭
preserved egg	*sōnghuā dàn*	松花蛋
salted duck egg	*xián yādàn*	咸鸭蛋
salted chicken egg	*xián jīdàn*	咸鸡蛋
pickles	*xiáncài*	咸菜

Western-style

coffee	*kāfēi*	咖啡
milk	*niúnǎi*	牛奶
bacon	*xiánròu*	咸肉
sausage	*xiāngcháng*	香肠
boiled egg	*zhǔ jīdàn*	煮鸡蛋
fried egg	*jiān jīdàn*	煎鸡蛋
scrambled eggs	*chǎo jīdàn*	炒鸡蛋
bread	*miànbāo*	面包
toast	*kǎo miànbāo*	烤面包
butter	*huángyóu*	黄油
jam	*guǒjiàng*	果酱
sugar	*táng*	糖

Cooking methods and common combinations

shredded …	… sī	…丝
diced …	… dīng	…丁
sliced …	… piàn	…片
… balls	… wán	…丸
… chunks/pieces	… kuài	…块
stir-fry …	chǎo …	炒…
barbecued …	chāshāo …	叉烧…
deep-fried …	jiān / zhá…	煎/炸…
crispy deep-fried …	xiāngsū …	香酥…
steamed …	qīngzhēng …	清蒸…
stewed …	dùn …	炖…
pot-stewed … in soy sauce	lǔ … /jiàng …	卤…/酱…
smoked …	xūn …	熏…
… with five spices	wǔxiāng …	五香…
… braised in soy sauce	hóngshāo …	红烧…
… braised in earthenware casserole	shāguō dùn …	沙锅炖…
sautéed …	yóumèn …	油焖…
stir-fried … with peanuts and chilli	gōngbǎo …	宫宝…
stir-fried … with chilli, ginger and garlic	yúxiāng …	鱼香…
stir-fried … with sauce added	huáliū …	滑溜…
… quick-fried with bean sauce	jiàng bào …	酱爆…
… quick-fried with spring onion	cōng bào …	葱爆…
… quick-fried in sesame paste	májiàng chǎo …	麻酱炒…
home-style …	jiācháng …	家常…
… with chilli and Sichuan pepper	málà …	麻辣…
curry …	gālí …	咖喱…
roast …	kǎo …	烤…

sweet and sour ...	*tángcù* ...	糖醋...
'three fresh' (usually meat with seafood) ...	*sānxiān* ...	三鲜...
... with tomato sauce	*fānqié zhī* ...	番茄汁...
... with oyster sauce	*háoyóu* ...	蚝油...
... in hot pot	*huǒguō* ...	火锅...

Soups

shark's fin soup	*yúchì tāng*	鱼翅汤
'three fresh' soup (usually, meat, prawns and a vegetable)	*sānxiān tāng*	三鲜汤
dried shrimp and seaweed soup	*háimǐ zǐcài tāng*	海米紫菜汤
shredded pork and pickled mustard greens soup	*zhàcài ròu sī tāng*	榨菜肉丝汤
hot and sour bean curd soup	*suānlà dòufu tāng*	酸辣豆腐汤
spinach and vermicelli soup	*bōcài fěnsī tāng*	菠菜粉丝汤
winter marrow soup	*shíjǐn dōngguā tāng*	什锦冬瓜汤
tomato and egg soup	*xīhóngshì jīdàn tāng*	西红柿鸡蛋汤
sliced pork and seasonal vegetable soup	*shícài ròu piàn tāng*	什菜肉片汤
Chinese mushrooms with sliced pork soup	*dōnggū ròu piàn tāng*	冬菇肉片汤

Pork, beef and lamb

pork	*zhūròu*	猪肉
steamed pork with rice	*fěn zhēng ròu*	粉蒸肉
pork belly braised in soy sauce	*hóngshāo ròu*	红烧肉
pork steamed first then stir-fried with chilli	*huí guō ròu*	回锅肉
'lion's head' (minced pork balls in gravy)	*shīzi tóu*	狮子头

'ants climbing the tree' (minced pork with vermicelli)	*máyi shàngshù*	蚂蚁上树
'bear's feet' (pig's feet braised in soy sauce)	*xióng zhǎng (zhū tí)*	熊掌(猪蹄)
stir-fried shredded pork with chilli, ginger and garlic	*yúxiāng ròu sī*	鱼香肉丝
sweet and sour spare ribs	*tángcù páigǔ*	糖醋排骨
stir-fried sliced pork with eggs, black fungus and dried lily	*mùxū ròu*	木须肉
barbecued pork	*chāshāo ròu*	叉烧肉
stir-fried diced pork with chilli	*làzi ròu dīng*	辣子肉丁
stir-fried sliced pork with bamboo shoots	*sún chǎo ròu piàn*	笋炒肉片
beef	*niúròu*	牛肉
deep-fried, shredded beef with five spices	*wǔ xiāng gānbiān niúròu sī*	五香干鞭牛肉丝
pot-stewed beef in soy sauce	*lǔ/jiàng niúròu*	卤/酱牛肉
stewed beef with five spices	*wǔ xiāng niúròu*	五香牛肉
shredded beef quick-fried with spring onions	*cōng bào niúròu sī*	葱爆牛肉丝
beef with oyster sauce	*háoyóu niúròu*	蚝油牛肉
lamb / mutton	*yángròu*	羊肉
lamb kebabs	*yángròu chuàn*	羊肉串
Mongolia hot pot	*shuàn yángròu*	涮羊肉
shredded lamb quick-fried with spring onions	*cōng bào yángròu sī*	葱爆羊肉丝
braised lamb with pancake	*yángròu pào mó*	羊肉泡馍

Chicken and duck

chicken	*jī*	鸡
crispy deep-fried chicken	*xiāngsū jī*	香酥鸡
sliced cold chicken	*bái zhǎn jī*	白斩鸡
stir-fried diced chicken with peanuts and chilli	*gōngbǎo jī dīng*	宫宝鸡丁
'beggar's chicken' (charcoal-baked marinated chicken)	*jiàohuā jī*	叫化鸡
duck	*yā / yāzi*	鸭/鸭子
Beijing roast duck	*Běijīng kǎo yā*	北京烤鸭
steamed salted duck	*xián shuǐ yā*	咸水鸭
crispy deep-fried duck	*xiāngsū yā*	香酥鸭
duck's feet with Chinese mushrooms	*xiānggū yā zhǎng*	香菇鸭掌

Fish and seafood

fish	*yú*	鱼
stir-fried fish slices with sauce	*huáliū yú piàn*	滑溜鱼片
sweet and sour fish	*tángcù yú kuài*	糖醋鱼块
steamed carp	*qīngzhēng lǐyú*	清蒸鲤鱼
fish braised in soy sauce	*hóngshāo yú*	红烧鱼
fish head stewed with bean curd	*yú tóu dùn dòufu*	鱼头炖豆腐
stir-fried shrimps with egg white	*fúróng xiārén*	芙蓉虾仁
sautéed king prawns	*yóumèn dàxiā*	油焖大虾
sautéed lobsters	*yóumèn lóngxiā*	油焖龙虾
paddyfield eel	*huángshàn*	黄鳝
stir-fried shredded paddyfield eel	*chǎo shàn sī*	炒鳝丝
steamed crab	*qīngzhēng pángxie*	清蒸螃蟹
stir-fried squid	*chǎo yóuyú*	炒鱿鱼
sea cucumber	*hǎishēn*	海参
jellyfish with cucumber (cold)	*hǎizhé bàn huánggua*	海蜇拌黄瓜

Vegetables and bean curd

vegetable	shùcài	蔬菜
stir-fried bean sprouts	chǎo dòuyá	炒豆芽
stir-fried seasonal vegetables	chǎo shí cài	炒时菜
stir-fried dwarf beans with bamboo shoots	dōngsǔn chǎo biǎndòu	冬笋炒扁豆
stir-fried mushrooms with fresh peas	xiānmó chǎo wāndòu	鲜蘑炒豌豆
aubergines with chilli, ginger and garlic	yúxiāng qiézi	鱼香茄子
stir-fried Chinese garlic chives with egg	jiǔhuáng chǎo jīdàn	韭黄炒鸡蛋
stir-fried tomato with egg	xīhóngshì chǎo jīdàn	西红柿炒鸡蛋
bean curd with chilli and Sichuan pepper	málà dòufu	麻辣豆腐
bean curd braised in earthenware casserole	shāguō dùn dòufu	沙锅炖豆腐
dried soy bean cream sheets	dòufu pí	豆腐皮
dried bean curd with five spices	wǔ xiāng dòufu gān	五香豆腐干
dried soy bean cream shreds	dòufu sī	豆腐丝
assorted gluten with bamboo shoots	sù shíjǐn	素什锦

Dessert

'eight treasures' (rice pudding with nuts, dates, etc.)	bābǎo fàn	八宝饭
sweet dumplings made with glutinous rice flour	yuánxiāo/tāngyuán	元宵/汤圆
almond tofu	xìngrén dòufu	杏仁豆腐
toffee apples	básī píngguǒ	拔丝苹果

Shopping

▮ All department stores and shops open seven days a week, usually from between 8.30 and 9 a.m. until 6 or 8 p.m. Some large department stores, especially in the south, stay open until 10 p.m.

▮ Prices are fixed in department stores and state-run shops, but in privately-owned shops it is normal to bargain.

▮ There are many **zìyóu shìchǎng** (market places) where individual stalls are put together. They sell almost everything. Fresh food and vegetable markets are sometimes separated from markets selling goods for daily use. Stall-holders in market places expect buyers to bargain with them, which makes your shopping interesting and fun. It also gives you an opportunity to practise your Chinese (imagine bargaining in Chinese)!

▮ It is very common in China to buy a piece of fabric and take it to a tailor's shop to have your clothes made. You can find tailor's shops very easily; some tailors have their stalls in market places. They are efficient and inexpensive.

▮ Supermarkets are relatively new in China. Chinese people go to **fùshí diàn** (sometimes called **cài shìchǎng**) or market places to buy food: fresh and cooked meat, fish, vegetables, soy bean-based products, etc.

▮ Most shops are not self-service; you need to deal with **shòuhuòyuán** (shop assistants). To attract the attention of a shop assistant, you can use **xiǎojie** to address a woman and **xiānsheng** to address a man (the term **tóngzhì**, meaning 'comrade', was used for this purpose in the old days and can still be heard occasionally). Payment is always made in cash except in some large Friendship Stores.

▮ **Yǒuyì Shāngdiàn** (Friendship Stores) can be found in some big cities. They were originally set up for visiting and resident foreigners in the early 1980s when demand exceeded supply in other shops. Although Friendship Stores are no longer places to buy things that can't be found in other shops (which was the case before), they are still full of good quality souvenirs which appeal to Westerners. Shops in luxury hotels and so-called 'Art and Craft Stores' also have very good souvenir items. It would be extremely difficult to get a refund in most shops, so make sure that what you buy is to your satisfaction when you buy it. Locally-made products are relatively inexpensive but imported goods such as coffee can be more expensive than in the West.

■ Note that films are sold in department stores and camera shops, not at the chemist. There is one English-language newspaper in China called 'The China Daily' which can be bought from bookshops, post offices or news-stands. Foreign newspapers are only available from luxury hotels.

■ In Beijing, the two main shopping areas are **Wángfújǐng** and **Xīdān** (both are near Tian'anmen Square). In Shanghai, the main shopping area is **Nánjīng Xī Lù**.

You may see

百货商店	bǎihuò shāngdiàn	department store
友谊商店	Yǒuyì Shāngdiàn	Friendship Store
工艺美术商店	Gōngyì Měishù Shāngdiàn	Art and Craft Store
书店	shūdiàn	bookshop
药店	yàodiàn	pharmacy
服装店	fúzhuāng diàn	clothing shop
鞋帽店	xiémào diàn	shoe and hat shop
食品店	shípǐn diàn	food shop
水果店	shuíguǒ diàn	fruit shop
自由市场	zìyóu shìchǎng	market
超级市场	chāojí shìchǎng	supermarket
副食店	fùshí diàn	food and vegetable shop
丝绸店	sīchóu diàn	silk shop

理发店	*lǐfà diàn* (for men)	barber's shop
发廊	*fàláng* (for both men and women)	hairdresser
裁缝店	*cáifeng diàn*	tailor's shop
报亭	*bàotíng*	news-stand

Useful words

go shopping	*mǎi dōngxi*	too expensive	*tài guì le*
to buy	*mǎi*	good bargain	*hésuàn*
to sell	*mài*	inexpensive	*piányi*
How much is it?	*Duō shǎo qián?*		

You may want to say

General phrases

Excuse me	*Duìbùqǐ*
Is there a ... near here?	*Fùjìn yǒu ... ma?*
... silk shop ...	*... sīchóu diǎn ...*
... camera shop ...	*... zhàoxiàng qìcái shāngdiàn ...*
... barber's shop ...	*... lǐfà diǎn ...*
... hairdresser ...	*... fàláng ...*
... tailor's shop ...	*... cáifeng diàn ...*
What time do you ...?	*Nǐmen jǐ diǎn ...?*
... open	*... kāimén ...*
... close	*... guānmén ...*
Do you sell ...?	*Nǐmen yǒu ... ma?*
... batteries	*... diànchí ...*
... shampoo	*... xǐfàyè ...*
... stamps	*... yóupiào ...*

Where can I buy …?	*Wǒ zài nǎr kéyi mǎi dào …?*
… suitcases	*… xiāngzi*
… cameras	*… zhàoxiàngjī*
… films	*… jiāojuǎn*
… an umbrella	*… yúsǎn*
I'm just browsing	*Wǒ kànkan*
Can you wrap it up, please?	*Nǐ kéyi bǎ zhège bāo yíxià ma?*
A carrier bag, please?	*Qǐng géi wǒ yí ge sùliào dài*
I'll take it	*Wǒ yào le*
I'll come back later	*Wǒ huítóu zài lái*
I need to think about it	*Wǒ xūyào xiǎngxiang*

Buying clothes or shoes

Could I have a look at that … one?	*Wǒ kéyi kàn yíxià nàge … de ma?*
… red …	*… hóng …*
… black …	*… hēi …*
… blue …	*… lán …*
… green …	*… lǜ …*
… yellow …	*… huáng …*
… white …	*… bái …*
… purple …	*… zǐ …*
… pink …	*… fěnhóng …*
… grey …	*… huī …*
I'd like a silk tie/scarf in …	*Wó xiǎng yào yī tiáo … de zhēn sī lǐngdài / wéijīn*
… a dark blue colour	*… shēn lán sè …*
… a light grey colour	*… qiǎn huī sè …*
Do you have any other colours?	*Nǐmen hái yǒu biéde yánsè de ma?*
Do you have more of this?	*Tóngyàng de hái yǒu ma?*

Have you got this in ...?	*Nǐmen yǒu ... hào de ma?*
... extra large	*... tè dà ...*
... large	*... dà ...*
... medium	*... zhōng ...*
... small	*... xiǎo ...*
I wear size 40 (for shoes)	*Wǒ chuān sìshí hào de xié*
Can I try it/them on?	*Wǒ kéyi shìshi ma?*
Is there a mirror?	*Yǒu jìngzi ma?*
It's/They're too ...	*Tài ...*
... big	*... dà le*
... small	*... xiǎo le*
... long	*... cháng le*
... short	*... duǎn le*
Have you got anything less expensive?	*Hái yǒu piányi yìxiē de ma?*
Will it shrink?	*Suō shuǐ ma?*
Will the colour fade?	*Tuì yánsè ma?*
Is it ...?	*Zhè shì ... ma?*
... pure silk	*... zhēn sī ...*
... 100% cotton	*... chún mián ...*
... leather	*... pí de ...*
... silver	*... yín de ...*
... linen	*... yàmá ...*

Buying daily neccessities

I'd like ...	*Wǒ yào ...*
... three rolls of film	*... sān ge jiāojuǎn*
... a black and white film for slides	*... yī ge hēi bái huàndēng jiāojuǎn*
... a colour film for slides	*... yī ge cǎisè huàndēng jiāojuǎn*
... two of those batteries	*... liǎng ge zhè zhǒng diànchí*
... a tube of toothpaste	*... yī tǒng yágāo*

... a cake of soap	... yí kuài xiāngzào
... some razor blades	... yìxiē dāo piàn
... a nail clipper	... yí ge zhījia dāo
... today's 'China Daily'	... jīntiān de Zhōngguó Rìbào
... a map of Beijing	... yì zhāng Běijīng dìtú

Buying food

Meat, vegetables and fruit are usually sold by **jīn** (exactly half a kilo) and there are 10 **liǎng** in one **jīn**.

I'd like ...	Wǒ xiǎng mǎi ...
... half a kilo of apples	... yì jīn píngguǒ
... a quarter of a kilo of lychees	... bàn jīn lìzhī
... two loaves of bread	... liǎng ge miànbāo
... three tins of Cola	... sān guàn kělè
... four bottles of beer	... sì píng píjiǔ
Have you got any ...?	Nǐmen yǒu ... ma?
... bananas	... xiāngjiāo ...
... oranges	... chéngzi ...
... pears	... lízi ...
... strawberries	... cǎoméi ...
... milk	... niúnǎi ...
... ice cream	... bīngjilíng ...

Bargaining and payment

How much is it ...?	Duō shǎo qián ...?
... per half kilo	... yì jīn
... per pack	... yì bāo
... per metre (for fabric)	... yì mǐ
... per box	... yì hé
It's too expensive	Tài guì le

What if I buy three of them?	*Rúguǒ wǒ mǎi sān ge ne?*
Would you accept 80 *yuan*?	*Bāshí kuài xíng ma?*
I won't take it	*Wǒ bú yào*
How much is it to have a Mao jacket made? *	*Zuò yī jiàn Zhōngshān zhuāng duō shǎo qián?*
Do you take traveller's cheques?	*Nǐmen shōu lǚxíng zhīpiào ma?*
Sorry, I don't have any change	*Duìbùqǐ, wǒ méiyǒu língqián*
Can I have a receipt, please?	*Qǐng gěi wǒ yī zhāng shōujù, hǎo ma?*

* The Chinese term for 'Mao jacket' is *Zhōngshān zhuāng*, which is named after Dr. Sun Yatsen, the founder of the first Chinese republic, whose other given name is *Zhōngshān*.

You may hear

Nín xiǎng mǎi shénme?	Can I help you? (in shops only)
Yǒu, zài nà biān	Yes, we have. It's over there
Duìbùqǐ, méi yǒu	Sorry, we haven't got any
Duìbùqǐ, mài guāng le	Sorry, it's sold out
Míngtiān dào xīn huò	We'll have the new stock tomorrow
Nín kéyǐ shìshi duìmiàn nàge shāngdiàn	You can try the shop opposite us
Yǒu zhège shìyàng de, méi yǒu zhè zhǒng yánsè	We have got some more in the same style but not this colour
Nánde chuān háishi nǚde chuān?	For a man or a woman?
Nín yào shénme yánsè?	What colour would you like?
Nín yào jǐ hào de?	Which size would you like?
Nín xiǎng shìshi ma?	Would you like to try it on?
Nín yào duō shǎo?	How many/much would you like?
Yí ge shí kuài, liǎng ge shíwǔ kuài	Ten *yuan* for one, and 15 *yuan* for two
Yìdiǎnr dōu bú guì	Not expensive at all
Zhìliàng hén hǎo	Very good quality

Zhè shì zuì dī jià	This is my lowest offer
Bù fēnkāi mài	They are not sold separately
Xíng ma?/Xíng bù xíng?	Is it all right?/Is it OK?
Nǐ yào ma?	Would you like to take it?
Hái yào biéde ma?	Anything else?
Duìbùqǐ, zhǎo bù kāi	Sorry, I have no change
Wǒmen yǐjing guānmén le	We are closed now

Sightseeing

■ General information on sightseeing and tourism can be obtained from **Guójì Lǚxíngshè, Guólǚ** for short (The China International Travel Service, CITS for short), which is the official organisation that deals with foreign tourists in China. CITS has offices in all the main cities and resorts and usually has a desk in tourist hotels. CITS also makes travel arrangements such as booking air and train tickets, and organising tours for foreign tourists.

■ Sightseeing tours by coach with English-speaking guides are also organised by CITS. They have one-day and two-day excursions to several places. You can make bookings at the CITS desk at your hotel. If none of the existing programmes interests you, talk to someone from the CITS to arrange a visit that does, but do remember to negotiate the fee first.

■ You almost always have to pay to visit museums, palaces and historical parks. These places are usually open every day, including weekends and public holidays, but some may close for one day during the week. The opening hours are generally the same as government office hours (i.e. 8.30 a.m. to 5.30 p.m.).

■ The part of the Great Wall that is close to Beijing is called **Bādálǐng**, and it is also the best preserved part, with wonderful views.

■ If you want to take pictures of local people, always ask for their permission. It helps if you offer to pay a small fee.

■ Do not sit or walk on the grass in public parks – there is a penalty for doing so.

■ In many tourist places, you'll find a rest-room for foreign travellers. Take advantage of it as the toilets there are usually much cleaner than public toilets.

You may see

开门	*kāimén*	open
关门	*guānmén*	closed
不准入内	*bù zhǔn rù nèi*	no entry
不准照相	*bù zhǔn zhàoxiàng*	no photography
请勿吸烟	*qǐng wù xīyān*	no smoking
请勿触摸	*qǐng wù chùmō*	Please do not touch
入口	*rùkǒu*	entrance
出口	*chūkǒu*	exit
一日游	*yī rì yóu*	one-day excursion
两日游	*liǎng rì yóu*	two-day excursion
长城	*Chángchéng*	the Great Wall
八达岭	*Bādálǐng*	Badaling
外宾售票处	*wàibīn shòupiào chù*	ticket office for foreigners
外宾休息室	*wàibīn xiūxīshì*	rest-room for foreigners
免费入内	*miǎnfèi rù nèi*	free admission

Useful words

tourist coach	*lǚyóu chē*
CITS	*Guójì Lǚxíngshè/Guólǚ*
tourist guide	*dǎoyóu*
visit	*cānguān*
museum	*bówùguǎn*
place of interest	*míngshèng gǔjī*

You may want to say

Information

Is there a CITS desk in this hotel?	*Zhège fàndiàn yǒu Guólǚ fúwùtái ma?*
Are there any tourist coaches to …?	*Yǒu qù … de lǚyóu chē ma?*
… the Great Wall	*… Chángchéng*
… the Ming Tomb	*… Shísān líng*
Are there any one-day excursions?	*Yǒu yì rì yóu ma?*
What time does the coach leave?	*Jǐ diǎn fāchē?*
What time does it get back?	*Jǐ diǎn huílai?*
Where does it leave from?	*Cóng nǎr chūfā?*
Can you pick us up from our hotel?	*Nǐ kéyi lái fàndiàn jiē wǒmen ma?*
How much is it?	*Duō shǎo qián?*
Is lunch included in the price?	*Bāokuò wǔfàn ma?*
I'd like to visit Beidaihe	*Wǒ xiǎng qù Běidàihé*
What's the best way to get there?	*Zěnme qù zuì hǎo?*
How many days do I need there?	*Wǒ zài nàr xūyào duō shǎo tiān?*
I can only stay for one day	*Wǒ zhǐ néng dāi yī tiān*
What are the places I must see?	*Yǒu shénme shì bìxū kàn de?*
Can I visit the Great Hall of the People?	*Wǒ kéyi cānguān Rénmín Dàhuìtáng ma?*
What days does it open?	*Nǎ jǐ tiān kāimén?*
What time does it open?	*Jǐ diǎn kāimén?*
What time does it close?	*Jǐ diǎn guānmén?*
Do you have an English-speaking guide?	*Nǐmen yǒu huì shuō Yīngwén de dǎoyóu ma?*
Do I have to pay for it?	*Xūyào fùqián ma?*
How much is it?	*Duō shǎo qián?*

113

Visiting places

One ticket, please	*Yī zhāng piào*
Two adults and one child	*Liǎng zhāng chéngrén piào, yī zhāng xiǎohái piào*
Have you got a map of this place?	*Yǒu zhèlǐ de dǎoyóu tú ma?*
I'd like one (map)	*Wǒ yào yī zhāng*
Can I take photos?	*Wǒ kéyǐ zhàoxiàng ma?*
Can I use a flash?	*Wǒ kéyǐ yòng shǎnguāngdēng ma?*
Could I take a photo of you?	*Wǒ kéyǐ géi nǐ zhào zhāng xiàng ma?*
Could you take a photo of me?	*Nǐ kéyǐ géi wǒ zhào zhāng xiàng me?*
Is there a rest-room for foreigners?	*Zhèr yǒu wàibīn xiūxishì ma?*
Where is …?	*… zài nǎr?*
… the toilet	*Cèsuǒ …*
… the exit	*Chūkǒu …*

You may hear

Duìbùqǐ, Guólǚ zài zhèr méi yǒu dàibiǎo	Sorry, we don't have CITS representatives here
Nǐ kéyǐ dǎ zhège diànhuà	You can phone this number
Duìbùqǐ, Guólǚ de rén xiàbān le	Sorry, CITS's staff have finished their work for the day
Nǐ yǒu shénme shì?	Is there anything I can do?
Míngtiān zǎoshang bā diǎn chūfā	It sets off at 8 o'clock tomorrow morning
Qǐng zài … děng	Please wait …
… dàmén wài …	… outside the entrance gate
… dàtīng li …	… in the lobby
Yígòng yī bǎi wǔshí yuán	One hundred and fifty *yuan* altogether
Bāokuò wǔcān hé ménpiào	Lunch and admission tickets are included in the price

*Duìbùqǐ, méi yǒu qù Běidàihé de
yī rì yóu*

Sorry, there is no one-day excursion
to Beidaihe

Nǐ děi zuò huǒchē

You've got to take a train

Nǐ xiǎng qù nǎr?

Where do you want to go?

Nǐ bìxū kànkan Gùgōng

You must visit the Palace Museum

Wǒmen měi tiān dōu kāimén

We open every day

Xīngqīyī bù kāimén

We don't open on Mondays

*Duìbùqǐ, suóyǒude dǎoyóu xiànzài
dōu hěn máng*

Sorry, all the guides are busy at the
moment

Nǐ kéyǐ děng bàn ge xiǎoshí ma?

Can you wait for half an hour?

▌ It's very likely that you will have interpreters helping you at meetings and around the negotiating table, but if you can speak some Chinese, it will definitely make a good impression on your Chinese partners and show you have made an effort and are taking the business seriously. You may also find it useful to know a few Chinese phrases to deal with situations when there aren't enough interpreters around, for example, at company receptions.

▌ Chinese companies usually arrange for interpreters. However, it's a good idea to take your own interpreter who understands both cultures if tough negotiating is expected.

▌ Titles are important in Chinese business circles. Job titles such as 'manager' and 'director' are used as forms of address as well as forms of reference. For example, if someone's surname is **Wáng** and s/he is a manager, s/he will be referred to as **Wáng jīnglǐ** (*lit.* Wang manager) and will be addressed in the same way. Thus it is very important that you find out not only the names of the people you are going to meet but also their job titles and positions in terms of seniority. When you meet your business partner(s) for the first time, always dress formally and exchange business cards after the hand-shaking. It's useful to have your business cards printed in both Latin script and Chinese characters. If you do not know how to say the person's title in Chinese, you can use their surname followed by i) **xiāngsheng** (Mr.) to address men; ii) **xiǎojie** (Miss) to address young women; or iii) **nǚshì** (Madam) to address older women. Once the initial formality is over and your Chinese partners' dealings become less formal, you should follow accordingly.

▌ During meetings or negotiations, if you get an evasive response such as 'It needs further consideration' or 'I need to talk to someone else', do not pursue the matter further. One thing you must not do is to make your Chinese partner lose face in front of his or her colleagues. You can always talk to him or her privately after the meeting and find out the real issue.

■ You will be very well looked after by your Chinese partners. Don't feel you are being organised; it is regarded as unfriendly to leave one's guests alone. A welcome banquet is usually held on the day of your arrival. The host always makes a welcome speech and expects the most senior person (in terms of work position) in the guest group to say something as well. It is very important that you bring some gifts from home with you so that you can give them to your business partners after the speech. Gift-giving is seen as a desire to start or maintain a good relationship. The gifts don't have to be expensive; things which are made by your company or represent your company or the place you come from will be fine. Gifts should be offered modestly by using polite expressions such as **bù chéng jìnyì** (*lit.* a small something not enough to show our respect), **qǐng xiào nà** (*lit.* please accept such a laughably small gift), etc. Clocks and knives are culturally inappropriate gifts as the phrase 'to give clocks' in Chinese sounds like 'to send someone to death' and giving someone a knife can be taken as a signal of ending a relationship.

■ You must also bear in mind that eating out is part of doing business, as lots of deals are closed at the dinner table. After you've been taken out a few times, it's a good idea to return the hospitality by inviting your business partners to a meal. Beware a drink called **bái jiǔ** (*lit.* white alcohol); it is very popular at dinner tables, has many brands and is very, very strong. If you have important business to discuss, it might be better to avoid the stuff. You can simply say that you do not drink and then toast with non-alcoholic drinks instead.

■ China is predominantly a relationship culture. It is very important to build up good **guānxì** (connections). If you are regarded by the Chinese as their **guānxì hù** (*lit.* connection client) or **lǎo guānxì** (*lit.* old connection), you have made it in business. In order to build up good business relations with your Chinese partner, you need first of all to build up a good personal relationship. This can be achieved by showing interest in your partner's family and work, taking him or her out for dinner, etc; and don't forget to chat in Chinese whenever you can!

■ Business hours in China are normally from 8 a.m. to 5 p.m. usually with a two-hour lunch break at 12 noon. In some cities where it is very hot in the summer, the lunch break in summer can be as long as three hours, as many Chinese people like to have a nap after lunch.

■ Government organisations and state-owned companies work from Monday to Friday. Joint-venture or private companies may have their own regulations and you can easily find out yourself.

You may see

合同	hétong	contract
部长	bùzhǎng	minister
总经理	zǒng jīnglǐ	managing director
经理	jīnglǐ	manager
副经理	fù jīnglǐ	deputy manager
厂长	chǎngzhǎng	manager (of a factory)
主席	zhǔxí	chairman
主任	zhǔrèn	director
总工程师	zǒng gōngchéngshī	chief engineer
销售部	xiāoshòu bù	sales department
人事部	rénshì bù	personnel department
广告部	guǎnggào bù	advertising department
会议室	huìyì shì	conference room

Useful words

business card	míng piàn
company	gōngsī
limited company	yǒuxiàn gōngsī
holdings	kònggǔ
headquarters	zǒngbù

Hong Kong office	*Xiāng Gǎng bànshìchù*
secretary	*mìshū*
collaboration	*hézuò*

First meeting and at the reception

Very pleased to meet you	*Hěn gāoxìng jiàndào nín*
How do you do?	*Nín hǎo*
My name is …	*Wǒ jiào …*
I work for the BBC	*Wǒ zài BBC gōngzuò*
Are you …?	*Nín shì … ma?*
… Mr. Li	*… Lǐ xiānsheng …*
… Miss Wang	*… Wáng xiǎojie …*
… Madam Zhang	*… Zhāng nǚshì …*
… Manager Zhao	*… Zhào jīnglǐ …*
… (factory) Manager Liu	*… Liú chángzhǎng …*
… the person in charge	*… fùzé rén …*
What should I call you?	*Wǒ gāi zěnme chēnghū nín?*
I'd like to see Mr. Wang in the International Sales Department	*Wǒ xiǎng jiàn yíxià Guójì Xiāoshòu Bù de Wáng xiānsheng*
I have an appointment with Miss Cheng in the Public Relations Department	*Gōng Guān Bù de Chéng xiǎojie yuē wǒ lái jiàn tā*
What time will he/she be back?	*Tā jǐ diǎn néng huílai?*
Can I wait here for a while?	*Wǒ zài zhèr děng yìhuǐr, xíng ma?*
Can I leave a message?	*Wǒ kéyi liú ge huà ma?*
Please give this note to him/her	*Qíng bǎ zhè zhāng tiáozi gěi tā*
On which days of the week do you work?	*Nǐmen měi zhōu ná jǐ tiān gōngzuò?*

119

Business meetings

Shall we have another meeting?	*Wǒmen zài kāi ge huì, hǎo ma?*
Where is the interpreter?	*Fānyì zài nǎr?*
Is Mr Wang coming?	*Wáng xiānsheng lái ma?*
Could you explain it again?	*Qǐng zài jiěshì yī biàn, hǎo ma?*
Have I understood it correctly?	*Wǒ zhème lǐjiě, duì ma?*
What do you think?	*Nǐ juéde zěnme yàng?*
Please consider the matter	*Qǐng kǎolǜ zhè jiàn shì*
Shall we talk it over again?	*Wǒmen zài tántan, hǎo ma?*
Is there anything you are not happy about?	*Yǒu shénme bù mǎnyì de dìfang ma?*
Are you ready to sign the contract?	*Nǐmen kéyi qiān hétong le ma?*
When are we going to sign the contract?	*Wǒmen shénme shíhou qiān hétong?*
Thank you for your understanding and support	*Xièxie nǐmende lǐjiě hé zhīchí*
I wish our collaboration every success	*Zhù wǒmen hézuò chénggōng*
I hope we'll meet again	*Xīwàng wǒmen hái huì jiànmiàn*
See you in London	*Lúndūn jiàn*

Working in China

Apart from going to China on short business trips, some people visit for longer periods of time to teach English, to represent a company, etc. Here are some useful phrases:

I'm here …	*Wǒ zài zhèr …*
… teaching English	*… jiāo Yīngwén*
… for a conference	*… kāihuì*
… on a lecture tour	*… jiǎngxué*
… studying Chinese	*… xué Zhōngwén*
I teach English at a university	*Wǒ zài yī ge dàxué jiāo Yīngwén*

Our company has an office in Beijing and I'm the chief representative	*Wǒmen gōngsī zài Běijīng yǒu ge bànshìchù, wǒ shì shǒuxí dàibiǎo*
I have been here for …	*Wǒ lái zhèr yǐjing … le*
… four weeks	*… sì ge xīngqī …*
… three months	*… sān ge yuè …*
… two years	*… liǎng nián …*
I'm staying for another six months	*Wǒ hái yào dāi liù ge yuè*
I'm staying for a year in total	*Wǒ yígòng dāi yī nián*

Social occasions

Please accept our small gift	*Qǐng shōuxià wǒmen de yìdiǎnr xīnyì*
Here is a little something – please accept it	*Zhè yǒu yìxiē xiǎo lǐwù, qǐng shōuxià*
You're too generous	*Nǐ tài kèqi le*
This must be very precious	*Zhè yídìng hěn guìzhòng*
This is beautiful	*Zhēn piàoliang*
Wonderful	*Tài hǎo le*
Let's drink to a successful collaboration	*Zhù hézuò chénggōng*
I don't drink	*Wǒ bù hē jiǔ*
Can I toast with orange juice?	*Wǒ yòng júzi zhī dàitì, xíng ma?*
Your good health	*Zhù nǐ shēntǐ jiànkāng*
Thank you for everything	*Xièxie nǐ wèi wǒmen zuò de yíqiè*
The dinner was superb	*Zhè dùn fàn fēicháng hǎo*
I'd like to take you out for a meal	*Wó xiǎng qǐng nǐ chī fàn*
Which restaurant would you like to go to?	*Nǐ xiǎng qù nǎ jiā cānguǎn?*
It's my treat	*Wó qǐng kè*

You may hear

Ní hǎo, yǒu shì ma?	Hello, can I help you?
Nín guì xìng?	What's your name?
Ní zhǎo shéi?	Whom are you looking for?
Ní shì nǎ ge gōngsi de?	Which company do you work for?
Huānyíng nǐ lái Zhōngguó	Welcome to China
Yílù shùnlì ma?	Did you have a good journey?
Ní xiǎng xiān xiūxi yìhuǐr ma?	Would you like to have a rest first?
Ràng wǒ jièshào yíxià	Let me introduce you
Ní kéyi géi wǒ yì zhāng nǐde míng piàn ma?	May I have your business card, please?
Ní zài Zhōngguó gàn shénme?	What are you doing in China?
Ní jiāo shénme?	What do you teach?
Ní lái Zhōngguó duō jiǔ le?	How long have you been in China?
Ní yào zài Zhōngguó dāi duō jiǔ?	How long are you going to stay in China?
Hǎo zhúyi	Good idea
Kàn qíngkuàng	It depends
Zhège jiànyì hén hǎo	It's a good suggestion
Wó kǎolù yíxià	I'll think about it
Yào qǐngshì yíxià	It needs permission from the top
Bù kěnéng	Impossible
Wǒ bù tóngyì	I disagree
Zhēn bàoqiàn	I'm terribly sorry
Wǒ chídào le	I'm late
Ràng nín jiú děng le	Sorry to have kept you waiting
Tā bú zài	He/She is not in
Tā zhèngzài kāihuì	He/She is in a meeting
Nín yuànyi děngdeng ma?	Would you like to wait?

▌ Almost every organisation in China, including hotels, has its own clinic, and doctors working at these clinics play the role of a general practitioner. A doctor working in the clinic will refer you to a hospital if the problem is serious. For minor problems, you can get medication from pharmacies, which sell only non-prescription medicines. You can get Western as well as traditional Chinese herbal medicine from almost all pharmacies. If a pharmacy only specialises in Chinese herbal medicine, it will be shown on the sign. Prescribed medicines can only be obtained from the clinic or hospital in which the doctor you see works. If there is no clinic in your hotel and you become ill, you should let your tourist guide or the hotel clerk know. They will be able to make arrangements for you to see a doctor who can speak English.

▌ If you are ill when travelling by yourself in a small town, you can always go to a **yīyuàn** (hospital). The sign for a hospital is a red cross against a white background. Dental services in China are found in local general hospitals.

▌ In Beijing, Shanghai and Guangzhou, there are hospitals where specialised clinics are set up to treat foreigners (see USEFUL ADDRESSES AND TELEPHONE NUMBERS). Foreign patients must pay for treatment costs and medication immediately. It is a good idea to get comprehensive insurance before leaving home.

▌ When Chinese people say things to you like 'You don't look very well' or 'You look a bit tired', it is to show their concern, so don't feel offended.

You may see

医院	*yīyuàn*	hospital
药店	*yàodiàn*	pharmacy

中药店	zhōng yàodiàn	Chinese herbal medicine shop
医务所	yīwùsuǒ	clinic
诊所	zhénsuǒ	clinic
外用药	wàiyòngyào	for external use
急诊部	jízhěn bù	emergency department
牙科	yákē	dentistry

Useful words

| doctor | yīshēng/dàifu | nurse | hùshi | ill | bìng le |

You may want to say

General phrases

… am/is ill	… bìng le
I …	Wǒ …
My wife …	Wǒde tàitai …
My husband …	Wǒde xiānsheng …
My friend …	Wǒde péngyou …
I don't feel well	Wǒ bù shūfu
Is there a clinic in the hotel?	Fàndiàn lǐ yǒu yīwùsuǒ ma?
Can you send for a doctor for me?	Nǐ kéyǐ tì wǒ jiào ge yīshēng ma?
I need to see a doctor	Wǒ xūyào kàn yīshēng
I need to see a dentist	Wǒ xūyào kàn yáyī
It's urgent	Hěn jí
Is there a hospital nearby?	Fùjìn yǒu yīyuàn ma?
Is there an English-speaking doctor?	Yǒu huì shuō Yīngwén de yīshēng ma?
Where is the pharmacy?	Yàodiàn zài nǎr?

At the doctor's

What's wrong with me?	*Wǒ dé le shénme bìng?*
Is it serious?	*Yánzhòng ma?*
I have high blood pressure	*Wó yǒu gāo xuěyā*
I suffer from insomnia	*Wǒ shī mián*
I have heart disease	*Wó yǒu xīnzàng bìng*
I'm diabetic	*Wó yǒu tángniào bìng*
I'm pregnant	*Wǒ huáiyùn le*
I'm allergic to ...	*Wǒ duì ... guòmǐn*
... herbal medicine	*... cǎo yào ...*
... aspirins	*... āsīpīlín ...*
... penicillin	*... qīngméisù*
I don't want to have an injection	*Wǒ bù xiǎng dǎzhēn*
How much is it going to cost?	*Yào huā duō shǎo qián?*
Where can I get the medicine?	*Zài nǎr ná yào?*

Symptoms

I have ...	*Wǒ ...*
... a headache	*... tóuténg*
... toothache	*... yáténg*
... stomach-ache	*... dùziténg/wèiténg*
... a temperature	*... fāshāo*
... diarrhoea	*... lādùzi*
... a sore throat	*... sǎngzi téng/hóulóng téng*
... difficulty breathing	*... chuǎn bú shàng qì*
... a cough	*... késou*
... chest pains	*... xiōngbù téng*
I feel ...	*Wǒ gǎnjué ...*
... dizzy	*... tóuyūn*
... nauseous	*... ěxīn*

... shivery	... fādŏu
My ... hurt(s)	Wŏ ... téng
... back ...	... bèi ...
... eyes ...	... yănjing ...
... chest ...	... xiōngbù ...
I can't move my ...	Wŏde ... bù néng dòng
... neck	... bózi ...
... wrist	... shŏuwàn ...
I'm constipated	Wŏ biànbì
I've got a rash	Wŏ chū pízhĕn le
I've got a nosebleed	Wŏ liú bíxuè le
It hurts here	Zhèr téng
It's very painful	Tèbié téng
I don't want to eat	Wŏ bù xiăng chī fàn
I've vomited	Wŏ tù le
I've injured my ...	Wŏ shuāi shāng le ...
... leg	... tuĭ
... ankle	... jiăo bózi
I've broken this part	Wŏ shuāi duàn le zhèr
I've been bitten by a dog	Wŏ bèi gŏu yăo le
I've been stung (by an insect)	Wŏ bèi (chóngzi) dīng le
There's a cavity down there	Lĭmian yŏu ge dòng
Do I need any fillings?	Wŏ xūyào bŭyá ma?
I don't want a filling put in	Wŏ bù xiáng bŭyá

At the pharmacy

I want to buy some ...	Wŏ xiáng măi yìxiē ...
... aspirins	... āsipilín
... painkillers	... zhĭténg yào
... antibiotics	... xiāoyán yào
... cold relief	... gănmào yào

... diarrhoea tablets	... zhǐxiè yào
... laxatives	... qīngxiè jì (xiè yào)
... cough medicine	... zhǐké yào
... throat lozenges	... qīnghóu yào
... sleeping pills	... ānmián yào
Do you have ...?	Nǐmen yǒu ... ma?
... plasters	... chuàngkětiē ...
... antiseptic	... xiāodú shuǐ ...
How do I apply it?	Zěnme yòng?
How many times a day do I take it?	Yì tiān chī jǐ cì?
How many tablets do I take each time?	Yí cì chī jǐ piàn?

You may hear

At the doctor's

Nǎr bù shūfu?	What is the problem?
Nǎr téng?	Where does it hurt?
Téng de lìhai ma?	Is it very painful?
Nǐ bìng le jǐ tiān le?	How long have you been feeling unwell?
Chī yào le ma?	Have you taken any medicine?
Nǐ duō dà le?	How old are you?
Gěi nǐ liáng yíxià ...	Let me take your ...
... tǐwēn	... temperature
... xuèyā	... blood pressure
Tīng yíxià nǐde xiōngbù	I need to listen to your chest
Shēn hūxī	Breathe deeply, please
Zài hūxī	Breathe again, please
Qǐng zhāngkāi zuǐ	Open your mouth, please
Shuō 'a'	Say 'ah'

Qǐng tǎng xià	Please lie down
Nǐ jīntiān chī shénme le?	What have you eaten today?
Nǐ duì shémen yào guòmǐn?	Are you allergic to any medicine?
Yào gěi nǐ …	I'm going to …
… dǎzhēn	… give you an injection
… pāi X-guāngpiàn	… send you for an X-ray
… bá yī ge yá	… take this tooth out
… bú liǎng ge yá	… give you two fillings
Wǒ xūyào gěi nǐ …	I need …
… yàn niào	… a urine sample
… yàn xuè	… a blood sample
Zhège yá xūyào bǔ	You need a filling
Nǐ shíwù zhòngdú le	You have food poisoning
Nǐ gǎnmào le	You've got the flu
Nǐde xuèyā piān gāo	Your blood pressure is a bit high
Nǐ xūyào qù yīyuàn	You will have to go to hospital
Méi guānxi	It's nothing serious
Wǒ gěi nǐ kāi yìxiē yào	I'll give you a prescription
Xiūxi jǐ tiān	Rest for a couple of days
Bú yào chī yóunì de	Don't eat greasy food

At the pharmacy and Dosage

Zhè shì wàiyòng yào	This is for external use
Měi tiān cā sān cì	Apply three times a day
Fàn hòu chī zhège yào	Take this medicine after meals
Fàn qián chī	Before meals
Shuì qián chī	Before going to bed
Měi tiān sān cì, měi cì yī piàn	One tablet three times a day

Parts of the body

ankle	*jiǎobózi*	heart	*xīnzàng*
appendix	*lánwěi*	heel	*jiǎogēn*
arm	*gēbo*	hip	*túnbù*
artery	*dòngmài*	intestine	*cháng*
back	*bèi*	jaw	*é*
bladder	*pángguāng*	kidney	*shènzàng*
blood	*xiě/xuè*	knee	*xīgài*
body	*quánshēn*	leg	*tuǐ*
bone	*gǔtou*	ligament	*rèndài*
bowel	*chángzi*	lip	*zuǐchún*
breast	*rǔfáng*	liver	*gānzàng*
buttocks	*túnbù/pìgu* (informal)	lung	*fèi*
cartilage	*ruǎngǔ*	mouth	*zuǐ*
chest	*xiōngbù*	muscle	*jīròu*
chin	*xiàba*	nail	*zhíjiǎ*
ear	*ěrduo*	neck	*bózi*
elbow	*gēbozhǒu*	nerve	*shénjīng*
eye	*yǎnjing*	nose	*bízi*
eyebrow	*méimao*	penis	*yīnjīng*
eyelash	*yǎnjiémáo*	rectum	*zhícháng*
face	*liǎn*	rib	*lèigǔ*
finger	*zhǐtou*	shoulder	*jiānbǎng*
foot	*jiǎo*	skin	*pífū*
genitals	*shēngzhíqì*	spine	*jǐzhuīgǔ*
gland	*xiàn*	stomach	*wèi*
hair (of head)	*tóufa*	tendon	*jiàn*
hair	*máo*	testicle	*gāowán*
hand	*shǒu*	thigh	*dàtuǐ*
head	*tóu*	throat	*hóulóng / sǎngzi*

thumb	*mǔzhǐ*	vagina	*yīndào*
toe	*jiǎozhǐtou*	vein	*jìngmài*
tongue	*shétou*	waist	*yāo*
tonsil	*biǎntáo tǐ / biǎntáo xiàn*	wrist	*shǒuwàn*
tooth	*yá*		

Diseases and related terms

AIDS	*àizībìng*	hyperthyroid	*jiǎzhuàngxiàn kàngjìn*
allergy	*guòmǐn*	insomnia	*shīmián*
anaphylaxis	*guòmǐnxìng*	leukemia	*báixuèbìng*
angina pectoris	*xīnjiǎoténg*	measles	*mázhěn*
appendicitis	*lánwěiyán*	miscarriage	*liúchǎn*
arthritis	*guānjiéyán*	muscle pain	*jīròu téng*
bronchial asthma	*zhīqìguǎn xiàochuǎn*	myocarditus	*xīnjīyán*
bronchitis	*zhīqìguǎnyán*	neuralgia	*shénjīngténg*
cancer	*áizhèng*	pneumonia	*fèiyán*
cold	*gǎnmào*	tuberculosis	*fèijiéhé*
diabetes	*tángniàobìng*	virus	*bìngdú*
diarrhoea	*lādùzi*	whiplash injury	*tóubù shòushāng*
encephalitis	*nǎoyán*		
flu	*liúgǎn*		
fracture	*gǔzhé*		
haemorrhage	*chūxuè*		
haemorrhoid	*zhìchuāng*		
hay fever	*huāfěn rè*		
heart attack	*xīnzàng bìng fāzuò*		
hepatitis	*gānyán*		
high blood pressure	*gāo xuèyā*		

Conversion tables

Length

English	Chinese pinyin	Chinese equivalent
centimetre(s)	*límĭ*	
metre(s)	*mĭ*	1 metre = 3 *chĭ*
kilometre(s)	*gōnglĭ*	1 kilometre = 2 *lĭ*

Area

English	Chinese pinyin	Chinese equivalent
square metre	*píngfāng mĭ*	
square kilometre	*píngfāng gōnglĭ*	
acre	*gōngmŭ*	1 acre = 0.15 *shìmŭ*
hectare	*gōngqĭng*	1 hectare = 15 *shìmŭ*

Weight

English	Chinese pinyin	Chinese equivalent
kilogram	*gōngjīn*	1 kilogram = 2 *jīn*
gram	*kè*	

National holidays and festivals

▌ Some public holidays in China have fixed dates but most Chinese festivals are calculated according to the lunar calendar and thus fall on different dates of the solar calendar (i.e. Western calendar) each year.

▌ Shops, theatres, cinemas and museums remain open on all public holidays and festivals. Business and government offices usually close for a week during Chinese New Year.

Fixed dates

1 January	New Year's Day	*Yuán Dàn/Xīn Nián*
1 May	Labour Day	*Láodòng Jié*
1 October	National Day	*Guóqìng Jié*

Unfixed dates

Late January or early February (1st day of the lunar calendar)
Spring Festival/Chinese New Year   *Chūn Jié/Xīn Nián*

Early February or late February (15 January on the lunar calendar)
Lantern Festival   *Yuánxiāo Jié*

Anytime in September (15 August on the lunar calendar)
Moon Festival/Mid Autumn Festival   *Zhōngqiū Jié*

Useful addresses and telephone numbers

Outside China

The Chinese Embassy
31 Portland Place
London W1N 3AG

Tel: 0171 636 5726

China National Tourist Office
4 Glentworth Street
London NW1 5PG

Tel: 0171 935 9427/9787

Air China
41 Grosvenor Gardens
London SW1W OBP

Tel: 0171 630 0919

China Travel Service and Information Centre
78 Shaftesbury Ave.
London W1V 7DG

Tel: 0171 439 8888

The Chinese Embassy
247 Federal Highway
Watson
Canberra, 2600 ACT
Australia

Tel: 06 273 4780

The Chinese Embassy
2300 Connecticut Avenue NW
Washington DC 20008
United States of America

Tel: 202 328 2500

Inside China

The British Embassy
11 Guanghua Lu
Jianguomenwai
Beijing
Tel: 010 6532 1961 (inside China)
Tel: +86 10 6532 1961 (from abroad)

The American Embassy
3 Xiushui Beijie
Jianguomenwai
Beijing
Tel: 010 6532 3831 (inside China)
Tel: +86 10 6532 3831 (from abroad)

China International Travel Service
6 Dong Chang'an Dajie
Beijing
Tel: 010 6512 1122

Air China
15 Chang'an Avenue West
Beijing
Tel: 010 6601 7755

24-hour English language information hotline: 010 6513 0828

China Eastern Airlines
At Shanghai Hongqiao Airport
Tel: 021 6255 8899

China Northwest Airlines
At Xi'an Xianyang Airport
Tel: 029 729 8727

British Airways
Room 210, 2nd Floor
SCITE Tower
22 Jianguomenwai
Beijing
Tel: 010 6512 4070

Northwest Airlines
Room 101- 103
Jianguo Hotel
Beijing
Tel: 010 6500 2481

International flight reservations: tel. 010 6601 6667
Internal flight reservations: tel. 010 6601 3336
Beijing's Capital International Airport: tel. 010 6456 3220/3221
Telephone directory enquiries for inside China: tel. 114
International telephone directory enquiries: tel. 116
Police emergency: tel. 110
Fire: tel. 119
International SOS Assistance: tel. 010 6500 3419
Beijing Emergency Medical Centre: tel. 120

Hospitals with medical clinics for foreigners
Xiehe Hospital in Beijing
Tel: 010 6512 7733ext 217 (Emergency, 24 hours)
             ext 251 (Foreigner's section)
Guangdong No. 1 People's Hospital in Guangzhou: tel 020 8333 3090
Shanghai No. 1 People's Hospital in Shanghai: tel 021 6324 0090

Survival Chinese

Hello	*Nǐ hǎo*	Pardon	*Duìbùqǐ*
Good morning	*Zǎoshang hǎo*	Say it slowly, please	*Qǐng màn diǎnr shuō*
Good night	*Wǎn ān*	Could you write it down here?	*Nǐ néng xiě zài zhèr ma?*
Goodbye	*Zàijiàn*		
See you later	*Huí jiàn*	What's this?	*Zhè shì shénme?*
See you tomorrow	*Míngtiān jiàn*		
Yes	*Shì de; Shì*	It's very nice	*Hén hǎo*
No	*Bú shì; Bù*	It's delicious	*Hén hǎochī*
Thank you	*Xièxie*	I don't want it	*Bú yào*
You're welcome	*Bú kèqi*	Do you have …?	*Nǐ yǒu … ma?*
I'm sorry	*Duìbùqǐ*	Where is/are …?	*… zài nǎr?*
It's all right (in response to 'I'm sorry')	*Méi guānxi*	Where is the toilet?	*Cèsuǒ zài nǎr?*
		How much is it?	*Duō shǎo qián?*
Excuse me	*Duìbùqǐ*	What time is it?	*Jǐ diǎn le?*
I don't understand	*Wǒ bù dǒng*	I'm ill	*Wǒ bìng le*
I speak very little Chinese	*Wǒ zhǐ huì shuō yìdiǎnr Zhōngwén*	I need help	*Wǒ xūyào bāngzhù*
Can you speak English?	*Nǐ huì shuō Yīngwén ma?*		

English	Pinyin	Characters
advertising department	*guǎnggào bù*	广告部
Air China	*Zhōngguó mínháng*	中国民航
air mail	*hángkōng*	航空
airport	*fēijīchǎng*	飞机场
airport bus	*mínháng bānchē*	民航班车
arrival (at airport)	*dàogǎng/dàodá*	到港/到达
arrival (at train station)	*dàozhàn*	到站
Art and Craft Store	*Gōngyì Měishù Shāngdiàn*	工艺美术商店
avenue	*dàjiē*	大街
Badaling (part of the Great Wall)	*Bādálǐng*	八达岭
baggage	*xíngli*	行李
bank	*yínháng*	银行
Bank of China	*Zhōngguó yínháng*	中国银行
bar	*jiǔbā*	酒吧
barber's shop (for men)	*lǐfà diàn*	理发店
bathroom	*wèishēng jiān*	卫生间
beef	*niúròu*	牛肉
Beijing/Peking	*Běijīng*	北京
bicycle for hire	*chūzū zìxíngchē*	出租自行车
boarding gate	*dēngjī kǒu*	登机口
bookshop	*shūdiàn*	书店
British Airways	*Yīngguó hángkōng gōngsī*	英国航空公司
bus	*gōnggòng qìchē*	公共汽车
bus stop	*gōnggòng qìchē zhàn*	公共汽车站
café	*kāfēi tīng*	咖啡厅

Cantonese cuisine	*Yuè cài*	粤菜
carriage/coach	*chē xiāng*	车厢
chairman	*zhǔxí*	主席
charges/rates	*fángjià*	房价
check-in (at airport)	*bànlǐ dēngjī shǒuxù*	办理登机手续
chicken	*jī*	鸡
chief engineer	*zǒng gōngchéngshī*	总工程师
Chinese dumplings (with meat and vegetable fillings)	*jiǎozi*	饺子
Chinese herbal medicine shop	*zhōng yàodiàn*	中药店
Chinese yuan	*Rénmín bì (yuán)*	人民币(元)
… [Chinese currency units]	*yuán/jiǎo/fēn*	元/角/分
… [Chinese currency units] (informal)	*kuài/máo/fēn*	块/毛/分
clinic	*zhénsuǒ*	诊所
closed	*guānmén*	关门
clothing shop	*fúzhuāng diàn*	服装店
conference room	*huìyì shì*	会议室
contract	*hétong*	合同
dentistry	*yákē*	牙科
department store	*bǎihuò shāngdiàn*	百货商店
departure (at aiport)	*lígǎng/líkāi*	离港/离开
departure (at train station)	*fāchē/kāichē*	发车/开车
deputy manager	*fù jīnglǐ*	副经理
destination	*mùdìdì*	目的地
dining car	*cān chē*	餐车
director	*zhǔrèn*	主任
domestic	*guónèi*	国内
double room	*shuāngrén fángjiān*	双人房间
duck	*yā*	鸭
east	*dōng*	东

eight	bā	八，捌
emergency department	jízhěn bù	急诊部
emergency exit	jǐnjí chūkǒu	紧急出口
enquiries	wènxùn chù	问询处
entrance	jìnkǒu	进口
entrance	rùkǒu	入口
exit	chūkǒu	出口
fast bus	kuài chē	快车
fast food	kuài cāndiàn	快餐店
first floor	èr céng	二层
five	wǔ	五，伍
food shop	shípǐn diàn	食品店
food and vegetable shop	fùshí diàn	副食店
for external use	wàiyòngyào	外用药
for hire	kòng/yǒukòng	空/有空
foreign exchange counter	wàihuì duìhuàn	外汇兑换
four	sì	四，肆
free admission	miǎnfèi rù nèi	免费入内
French franc	Fǎguó fǎláng	法国法郎
Friendship Store	Yǒuyì Shāngdiàn	友谊商店
fruit shop	shuíguǒ diàn	水果店
full	mǎn	满
ground floor	yī céng	一层
Guangzhou/Canton	Guǎngzhōu	广州
Guilin	Guìlín	桂林
hairdresser (for both men and women)	fàláng	发廊
hard-seat	yìng zuò	硬座
hard-sleeper	yìng wò	硬卧
hospital	yīyuàn	医院
hotel manager	fàndiàn jīnglǐ	饭店经理

information desk	*wènxún chù*	问询处
international	*guójì*	国际
international direct dialling	*guójì zhí bō*	国际直拨
international postal service	*guójì yóuzhèng*	国际邮政
international telephone	*guójì diànhuà*	国际电话
lamb	*yángròu*	羊肉
lane	*hútòng/xiàng*	胡同/巷
large dish	*dà pán*	大盘
left-luggage	*xínglǐ jìcún chù*	行李寄存处
letter box	*xìn tǒng*	信筒
Lhasa (in Tibet)	*Lāsā*	拉萨
lift	*diàntī*	电梯
luxury hotel	*bīnguǎn/fàndiàn*	宾馆/饭店
luxury hotel (in the south)	*jiǔdiàn*	酒店
manager	*jīnglǐ*	经理
manager (of a factory)	*chángzhǎng*	厂长
managing director	*zǒng jīnglǐ*	总经理
market	*zìyóu shìchǎng*	自由市场
medium	*zhōng pán*	中盘
Men (toilet)	*nán*	男
menu	*càidān*	菜单
mid-range hotel	*lúguǎn*	旅馆
mini-bus	*xiǎo gōnggòng qìchē*	小公共汽车
minister	*bùzhǎng*	部长
national direct dialling	*guónèi zhí bō*	国内直拨
news-stand	*bàotíng*	报亭
night bus	*yèbānchē*	夜班车
nine	*jiǔ*	九, 玖
no entry	*bù zhǔn rù nèi*	不准入内
no entry	*jìnzhǐ rù nèi*	禁止入内
no photography	*bù zhǔn zhàoxiàng*	不准照相

no smoking	*qǐng wù xīyān*	请勿吸烟
noodles	*miàn/miàntiáo*	面/面条
north	*běi*	北
number	*hào*	号
one-day excursion	*yī rì yóu*	一日游
open	*kāimén*	开门
optician	*yǎnjìng diàn*	眼镜店
parcels	*bāoguǒ*	包裹
passport control	*hùzhào jiǎnchá*	护照检查
pedestrian crossing	*rénxíng héngdào*	人行横道
personnel department	*rénshì bù*	人事部
pharmacy	*yàodiàn*	药店
platform	*zhàntái*	站台
Please do not disturb	*qǐng wù dárǎo*	请勿打扰
Please do not touch	*qǐng wù chùmō*	请勿触摸
pork	*zhūròu*	猪肉
Post and Telecommunications Office	*yóu diàn jú*	邮电局
Post Office	*yóu jú*	邮局
public phone	*gōngyòng diànhuà*	公用电话
rail ticket	*huǒchē piào*	火车票
railway station	*huǒchē zhàn*	火车站
reception	*fúwùtái*	服务台
rest-room for foreigners	*wàibīn xiūxishì*	外宾休息室
restaurant	*cānguǎn/fànguǎn*	餐馆/饭馆
restaurant (in a hotel)	*cāntīng*	餐厅
rice	*mǐfàn*	米饭
road	*lù*	路
sales department	*xiāoshòu bù*	销售部
seafood	*hǎixiān*	海鲜
seven	*qī*	七, 柒

Shanghai	*Shànghǎi*	上海
shoe and hat shop	*xiémào diàn*	鞋帽店
Sichuan cuisine	*Chuān cài*	川菜
silk shop	*sīchóu diàn*	丝绸店
single room	*dānrén fángjiān*	单人房间
six	*liù*	六，陆
slow bus	*màn chē*	慢车
small dish	*xiǎo pán*	小盘
small inn	*lǚshè*	旅社
soft-sleeper	*ruǎn wò*	软卧
soft-sleeper waiting-room	*ruǎn wò hòuchē shì*	软卧候车室
soup	*tāng*	汤
south	*nán*	南
spring rolls	*chūnjuǎn*	春卷
stamps	*yóupiào*	邮票
steamed buns with various fillings	*bāozi*	包子
Sterling	*Yīng bàng*	英镑
street	*jiē*	街
supermarket	*chāojí shìchǎng*	超级市场
tailor's shop	*cáiféng diàn*	裁缝店
taxi	*chūzūchē*	出租车
tea shop	*chá guǎn*	茶馆
telegram	*diànbào*	电报
Telegrams and Telephones	*diànbào diànhuà*	电报电话
telephone booth	*diànhuà tíng*	电话亭
ten	*shí*	十，拾
the Great Wall	*Chángchéng*	长城
three	*sān*	三，叁
ticket office	*shòupiào chù*	售票处
ticket office for foreigners	*wàibīn shòupiào chù*	外宾售票处

tofu (bean curd)	dòufu	豆腐
toilet	cèsuǒ	厕所
train number	chē cì	车次
tram	diànchē	电车
two	èr	二, 贰
two-day excursion	liǎng rì yóu	两日游
underground pass	dìxià tōngdào	地下通道
US dollar	Měi yuán	美元
vegetables	shūcài	蔬菜
way out	chūkǒu	出口
west	xī	西
Women (toilet)	nǚ	女
Xi'an	Xī'ān	西安

Dictionary

The tones marked in the Dictionary do not reflect the tone changes caused by surrounding tones except for the syllables that carry the neutral tone (see PRONUNCIATION GUIDE).

A

abdomen	*fùbù*
ability	*nénglì*
able	*néng*
about	*dàyuē, zuǒyòu*
above	*zài … shàng*
abroad	*guówài*
accept	*shōuxià, shōu*
accident	*shìgù*
accommodation	*zhùsù*
account	*zhàng, zhànghù*
accountant	*kuàijì*
ache	*téng*
actor, actress	*yǎnyuán*
acupuncture	*zhēnjiǔ*
adaptor	*duōlùchāzuò*
address	*dìzhǐ*
administration	*xíngzhèng*
admire	*xiànmù*
admission	*rùchǎng*
admission ticket	*ménpiào, rùchǎng quàn*
adopt (children)	*shōuyǎng*
… (opinion)	*cǎinà*
adult	*chéngrén*
(in) advance	*tíqián*
adventure	*màoxiǎn*
advertisement	*guǎnggào*
advise	*quàngào*
aeroplane	*fēijī*
afraid	*hàipà*
after	*… hòu*
afternoon	*xiàwǔ*
afterwards	*yǐhòu*
again	*zài*
against	*fǎnduì*
age	*niánlíng*
agency	*dàilǐ*
ago	*… qián*
agree	*tóngyì*
agriculture	*nóngyè*
air	*kōngqì*
Air China	*Zhōngguó mínháng*
air-conditioning	*kōngtiáo*
aircraft	*fēijī*
airline	*hángkōng gōngsī*
air mail	*hángkōng*

airport	*fēijīchǎng*	antiseptic	*xiāodúshuǐ*
airport bus	*mínháng bānchē*	antique	*gǔdǒng*
aisle	*zǒuláng*	anxious	*zhāojí*
alarm clock	*nàozhōng*	any	*rènhé*
alcohol	*jiǔ*	anything	*rènhéshì*
all	*suóyǒude*	apartment	*gōngyù*
allergic to	*duì … guòmǐn*	apologise	*dàoqiàn*
all right	*hái kěyi, hǎo de*	apologies	*bàoqiàn*
allow	*zhǔn*	apple	*píngguǒ*
alone	*dāndú*	appointment	*yuēhuì*
already	*yǐjing*	appoximately	*dàyuē*
also	*yě*	April	*sìyuè*
alter	*gǎi*	are	*shì*
although	*suīrán*	area code	*dìqū hào*
altogether	*yígòng*	argue	*zhēnglùn*
always	*zǒngshì*	arm	*gēbo*
am	*shì*	around	*zhōuwéi*
a.m.	*zǎoshang,*	arrival	*dàodá, dàozhàn*
	shàngwǔ	arrive	*dàodá, dào*
ambulance	*jiùhù chē*	art	*yìshù*
America	*Měiguó*	Art and Craft Store	*Gōngyì Měishù*
American (people)	*Měiguórén*		*Shāngdiàn*
… (adj)	*Měiguó*	Art Gallery	*Měishù Guǎn*
anaesthetic	*mázuì*	artist	*yìshùjiā*
and	*hé*	ashtray	*yānhuīgāng*
angry	*shēngqì*	ask	*wèn*
animal	*dòngwu*	at	*zài*
ankle	*jiǎobózi*	attack	*xíjī*
another	*lìnwài*	attractive	*piàoliang,*
answer	*huídá*		*xiyǐnrén*
antibiotics	*xiāoyányào*	August	*bāyuè*

aunt (father's sister)	gūgu
…(mother's sister)	yímā
… (father's younger brother's wife)	shēnshen
… (father's elder brother's wife)	bómǔ
… (mother's brother's wife)	jiùmā
Australia	Aòdàlìyà
Australian (people)	Aòdàlìyàrén
author	zuòjiā
automatic	zìdòng
autumn	qiūtiān
avenue	dàjiē
avoid	bìmiǎn
awake	xǐng le
awful	zāogāo

B

baby	yīng'ér
back (body)	bèi
… (adj & adv)	hòumian
backwards	luòhòu
bad	huài, zāogāo, bùhǎo
bad at …	bù hǎo
bag	bāo
… (small size)	dàizi
baggage	xíngli
bakery	miànbāo fáng
balance (account)	zhīchū pínghéng
ball	qiú
ballpoint pen	yuánzhū bǐ
bamboo	zhúzi
banana	xiāngjiāo
bank	yínháng
Bank of China	Zhōngguó yínháng
bar	jiǔbā
barber's	lǐfà diàn
barbecued	kǎo
bargain (n)	hésuàn
… (v)	tǎojià huánjià
bargain sale	dà shuǎi mài
baseball	bàngqiú
basement	dìxiàshì
bath (v)	xǐzǎo
bath towel	yùjīn
bathroom	wèishēng jiān
battery	diànchí
be back	huílai
be closed	guānmén
be open	kāimén
beach	hǎitān, shātān
bean curd	dòufu
beautiful	měilì
because	yīnwéi
become	dāng, chéngwéi
bed	chuáng
bed sheet	chuáng dān
bedroom	wòshì
beef	niúròu

beer	*píjiǔ*	blanket	*tǎnzi*
before	*cóngqián*	bleed	*liúxuè*
begin	*kāishǐ*	blister	*shuǐpào, pào*
beginner	*chūxuézhě*	blonde	*jīnfà nǚrén*
behind	*hòumian*	blood	*xuè, xiě*
Beijing Opera	*Jīn Jù*	blood pressure	*xuèyā*
believe	*xiāngxìn*	blood type	*xuèxíng*
belong	*shǔyú*	blow	*dǎjī*
below	*zài … xiàmian*	blue	*lánsè*
berth	*pù*	board (aeroplane)	*shàng (fēijī)*
beside	*zài … pángbiān*	board of directors	*dǒngshì huì*
besides	*zàishuō, chú cǐ zhīwài*	boarding gate	*dēngjī kǒu*
best	*zuìhǎo*	boat	*chuán*
better	*bǐ … hǎo*	boil	*shāokāi*
between	*zài … zhījiān*	boiled egg	*zhǔ jīdàn*
beware	*zhùyì, dāngxīn*	boiled rice	*bái mǐfàn*
Bible	*Shèngjīng*	boiling/boiled water	*kāi shuǐ*
bicycle	*zìxíngchē*	bomb	*zhàdàn*
bicycle for hire	*chūzū zìxíngchē*	bone	*gǔtou*
big	*dà*	book (n)	*shū*
bill	*zhàngdān*	… (v)	*dìng*
biology	*shēngwùxué*	bookshop	*shūdiàn*
bird	*niǎo*	boots	*xuēzi*
birthday	*shēngrì*	boring	*méi yìsi*
bit, a bit	*yìdiǎnr*	borrow	*jiè*
bite	*yǎo, dīng*	bottle	*píngzi*
bitter	*kǔ*	bottle-opener	*kāi píng dāo*
black	*hēisè*	bottom	*dǐ, zuìdǐxià*
black and white	*hēi bái*	bow (v)	*jūgōng*
blade	*dāopiàn*	bow tie	*huā lǐngjié*

bowl	*wǎn*	brothers and sisters	*xiōngdì jiěmèi*
box	*hézi*		
box lunch	*hé fàn*	browse	*kànkan*
boy	*nánhái*	bruise	*cāshāng*
boyfriend	*nán péngyou*	brush	*shuāzi*
brain	*dà'nǎo, nǎozi*	… (v)	*shuā*
braised	*hóngshāo*	bucket	*tǒng*
branch	*fēnzhī, fēnbù*	Budda	*fó*
brave	*yǒnggǎn*	Buddism	*fójiào*
bread	*miànbāo*	Buddist	*fójiàotú*
break down	*huài le*	Buddist temple	*fójiào sìyuàn*
breakfast	*zǎofàn*	budget	*yùsuàn*
breathe	*hūxī*	buffet	*zìzhùcān*
bridge	*qiáo*	build	*jiàn, gài*
… (game)	*qiáopái*	building	*dàlóu*
briefcase	*shǒutíxiāng*	bulb	*dēngpào*
bright	*liàng, míngliàng*	burnt	*jiāo le*
bring	*dàilái, dài*	bus	*gōnggòng qìchē*
Britain	*Yīngguó*	bus stop	*qìchē zhàn*
British (adj)	*Yīngguó*	business	*shēngyi, jīngshāng*
… (people)	*Yīngguórén*		
British Airways	*Yīngguó hángkōng gōngsī*	business card	*míng piàn*
		business-class	*shāngwù cāng*
		business trip	*chūchāi*
broadcasting	*bōyīn*	businessman/ woman	*shāngrén*
brochure	*shuōmíngshū*		
broken	*duàn le, shuāi duàn le*	busy	*máng*
		but	*dànshì*
broken-hearted	*shāng xīn*	butcher's	*ròu diàn*
brother (younger)	*dìdi*	butter	*huángyóu*
… (elder)	*gēge*	buttock	*túnbù*
brothers	*xiōngdì*	button	*kòuzi*

147

buy	*mǎi*	captain (of ship)	*chuánzhǎng*
by (the end of …)	*zài … zhīqián*	car	*chē, jiàochē*
by myself	*zìjǐ*	car park	*tíng chē chǎng*
		car wash	*xǐ chē*
		card	*pái, kǎ*

C

cabbage	*juǎnxīncài*	care (v)	*guānxīn*
café	*kāfēi tīng*	careful	*dāngxīn*
cake	*dàn'gāo*	careless	*cūxīn*
calculator	*jìsuànqì*	carpet	*dìtǎn*
call (v), be called	*jiào*	carriage (train)	*chēxiāng*
call (formal)	*chēnghū*	carrier bag	*sùliào dài*
calendar	*rìlì*	carrot	*húluóbo*
calligraphy	*shūfǎ*	carry	*dài, tí*
calm	*lěngjìng, chénzhuó*	carry on	*jìxù*
		cartoon	*dònghuàpiàn*
calm down	*bié zhāojí*	cash (n)	*xiànjīn*
camera	*zhàoxiàngjī*	… (v)	*duìhuàn xiànjīn*
camp site	*sùyíng dì*	cashier	*shōukuǎnrén*
can	*néng, huì*	cassette	*cídài*
can opener	*kāi guàntoudāo*	castle	*chéngbǎo*
Canada	*Jiānádà*	cat	*māo*
cancel	*qǔxiāo*	catalogue	*mùlù*
candle	*làzhú*	catch (e.g. thief)	*zhuā*
candy	*táng*	… (e.g. train)	*gǎn*
canteen	*cāntīng*	cauliflower	*càihuā*
Canton	*Guǎngdōng*	cause (reason)	*yuányīn*
Cantonese (dialect)	*Guǎngdōnghuà*	caution	*dāngxīn*
Cantonese cuisine	*Yuè cài*	cavity (teeth)	*dòng*
cap	*màozi*	ceasefire	*tínghuǒ*
capital (city)	*shǒudū*	ceiling	*tiānhuābǎn*
… (money)	*zījīn*	celebration	*qìngzhù*

celebrity	míngrén
cemetery	mùdì
centimetre	límǐ
central heating	nuǎnqì
centralisation	zhōngyāng jíquán
centre	zhōngxīn
century	shìjì
ceramics	táocí
certainly	dāngrán
certificate	zhèngshū
chain	liànzi
chair	yǐzi
chairman	zhǔxí
champagne	xiāngbīn
chance	jīhuì, jīyù
change (coin)	língqián
... (e.g. date)	gǎi
... (e.g. money)	huàn
change for ... (v)	huàn
changing room	gēngyī shì
character	rénwù
... (in a film)	
... (personality)	xìnggé
... (written script)	zì
charge (v)	shōufèi
charge: in charge	fùzé
charge the battery	chōngdiàn
charming	mírén
chat	liáotiān
cheap	piányi

cheat	piàn
check	jiǎnchá
...	cháchá
(e.g. dictionary)	
check in (n, v) (at airport)	bànlǐ dēngjī shǒuxù
check in (n, v) (at hotel)	bànlǐ zhùsù shǒuxù
check out (n, v)	bànlǐ líkāi shǒuxù
cheek	liǎnjiá
Cheers!	gānbēi
cheese	nǎilào
chef	chúshī
chemist's	yàodiàn
cheque	zhīpiào
cherry	yīngtáo
chess	xiàngqí
chest	xiōngbù
chestnut	máolìzi
chicken	jī
chief (adj)	zǒng, shǒuxí, zhǔyàode
child, children	háizi, xiǎohái
chilli	làjiāo, làzi
china	cíqì
China	Zhōngguó
China Daily	Zhōngguó Rìbào
Chinese (adj)	Zhōngguó
Chinese (language)	Zhōngwén, Hànyǔ
... (people)	Zhōngguórén

Chinese food	*Zhōng cān, Zhōngguó fàn*	classroom	*jiàoshì*
Chinese herbal medicine	*Zhōng cǎo yào*	clean	*gānjìng*
		… (v)	*dǎsǎo*
Chinese tea	*Zhōngguó chá*	clear	*qīngchǔ*
Chinese traditional medicine	*Zhōng yī*	clerk	*zhíyuán*
Chinese Sichuan pepper	*huājiāo*	clever	*cōngming*
		client	*kèhù*
		climate	*qìhou*
chips	*tǔdòutiáo*	climb	*pá*
chocolate	*qiǎokèlì*	clinic	*zhěnsuǒ, yīwùsuǒ*
choose	*tiāo, xuǎn*		
chopsticks	*kuàizi*	cloakroom	*cúnyīshì*
chore	*jiāwùshì*	clock	*zhōng*
Christian	*Jīdūjiào*	close (v)	*guān*
Christmas	*Shèngdàn jié*	… (e.g. shops)	*guānmén*
church	*jiàotáng*	clothing	*fúzhuāng, yīfu*
cigarette	*xiāngyān*	cloud	*yún*
cinema	*diànyǐngyuàn*	cloudy	*duōyún, yīntiān*
circle (n)	*yuánquān*	club	*jùlèbù*
… (v)	*quānchū*	coach (long-distance bus)	*chángtúchē*
CITS	*guójì lǚxíngshè, guólǚ*	… (of a train)	*chēxiāng*
		… (of sport)	*jiàoliàn*
citizen	*gōngmín*	coast	*hǎibiān*
city	*chéngshì*	coat hanger	*yī jià*
civil servant	*gōngwùyuán*	Coca-Cola	*kěkǒu kělè*
class (as a group)	*bān*	coconut	*yēzi*
… (e.g. maths class)	*kè*	coffee	*kāfēi*
		coffee shop	*kāfēi diàn*
… (social grouping)	*jiēcéng, jiējí*	coin	*yìngbì*
classical	*gǔdiǎn*	coin phone	*tóubì diànhuà*

coke	*kělè*
cold	*lěng*
... have a cold	... *gǎnmào*
cold relief	*gǎnmào yào*
collar	*lǐngzi*
colleague	*tóngshì*
collaboration	*hézuò*
collect (somebody)	*jiē*
... (something)	*qǔ*
collective	*jítǐ*
colour	*yánsè*
comb	*shūzi*
come	*lái*
comedy	*xǐjù*
comfortable	*shūfu*
comic	*huáji*
commemorative	*jìniàn*
commercial	*shāngyè*
... (ads)	*guǎnggào*
common	
... (ordinary)	*yìbān*
... (public)	*gōngyòng*
commute	*chéngchē*
compact disc	*jíguāng chàngpán*
company	*gōngsī*
compare	*duìbǐ, bǐ*
complain, complaint	*bàoyuàn, mányuàn*
completely	*wánquán*
complicated	*fùzá*

compromise (v)	*ràngbù*
compulsory	*bìxūde*
computer	*diànnǎo, jì suànjī*
condition	*tiáojiàn*
condom	*bìyùntào*
conference	*huìyì, dàhuì*
conference room	*huìyì shì*
confirm	*quèrèn*
congratulate	*zhùhè*
Congratulations!	*gōngxǐ*
conscious	*qīngxǐng*
conservative	*bǎoshǒu*
consider	*kǎolǜ*
constipation	*biànbì*
consul	*lǐngshì*
consulate	*lǐngshìguǎn*
consultant	*zīxúnrén*
contact (v)	*yǔ ... liánxì*
contact name	*liánxìrén*
continent	*zhōu*
continue	*jìxù*
contract	*hétong*
control	*kòngzhì*
convenient	*fāngbiàn*
conversation	*duìhuà, tánhuà*
convey	*zhuǎndá*
conveyor belt	*chuánsòng dài*
cook (chef)	*chúshī*
... (v)	*zuòfàn*
cookery	*pēngtiáo*

cool	liáng, liángkuai	… (female other than above)	biǎojiě (elder) biǎomèi (younger)
copy (n)	kǎobèi		
… (v)	chāo xiàlai	cover (n)	gàizi
corn	yùmǐ	… (v)	gàishang
corner	jiǎoluò	cow	mǔniú
correct (adj)	duì, zhèngquè	crab	pángxie
… (v)	gǎizhèng	cramp (disease)	jìngluán
corridor	zǒuláng	crash (e.g. car)	xiāngzhuàng
cosmetic	huàzhuāngpǐn	… (v)	yāsuì
cost (n)	fèiyòng	credit card	xìnyòng kǎ
… (v)	huā	crispy	cuì
cotton	miánhuā	cross (v)	guò
100% cotton	chúnmián	crossroads	shízì lùkǒu
cough	késou	crowded	yōngjǐ, jǐ
could	kěyǐ, néng	cry	kū
counselling	zīxún	cucumber	huángguā
count (numbers)	shǔ	cuff	xiùkǒu
… (on someone)	kào	cuisine	pēngtiáo
counter	guìtái	culture	wénhuà
countryside	nóngcūn	cup	bēizi
country	guójiā	cupboard	guìzi
couple (a pair)	yíduìr	cure (v)	zhìhǎo
… (married)	fūqī	currency	huòbì
courage	yǒngqì	curtain	chuānglián
cousin (father's brothers' sons)	tánggē (elder) tángdì (younger)	cushion	kàodiàn
		customer	gùkè
… (male, other than above)	biǎogē (elder) biǎodì (younger)	cut (v)	qiēkāi, qiē
… (father's brothers' daughters)	tángjiě (elder) tángmèi (younger)		

… (wound)	kǒuzi	declare	xuānbù
cycle, cycling (of bicycle)	qí zìxíngchē	deep	shēn
		deep-fry	zhá, jiān
D		defect	quēdiǎn
		definitely	yídìng, kěndìng
dad	bàba, diē	degree (angle)	jiǎodù
daily	měirì, měitiān	… (temperature)	dù
damage	sǔnhuài	… (university degree)	xuéwèi
damn!	zāogāo!		
damp	cháoshī	delay	tuīchí, yánchí
dance (n)	wǔdǎo	delicious	hǎochī, xiāng
… (v)	tiàowǔ	delivery	sòng, dì
danger	wēixiǎn	demonstration	yóuxíng
dangerous	wēixiǎnde	dentist	yáyī
dark	hēisè	dentistry	yákē
… ('dark blue')	shēn	depart	líkāi, fēnkāi
data	zīliào	department (academic)	xì
date	rìqī		
date of birth	chūshēng rìqī	… (corporate)	bùmén
daughter	nǚ'ér	department store	bǎihuò shāngdiàn
daughter-in-law	xífu, érxí		
day	tiān	departure (flight)	lígǎng, líkāi
day after tomorrow	hòu tiān	… (train)	fāchē, kāichē
day before yesterday	qián tiān	departure tax (airport)	jīchǎng fèi
dead	sǐle	depend	kào
deaf	lóng	… it depends	kàn qíngkuàng
deal (n)	jiāoyì	deposit (n)	yājīn
debt	zhài	describe	miáoshù, xíngróng
December	shí'èryuè		
decide, decision	juédìng	dessert	tiándiǎn

153

destination	*mùdìdì, zhōngdiǎn*	disappointing	*shīwàngde*
		disease	*bìng*
detail (n)	*xìjié*	dish (bowl)	*wǎn*
detailed	*xiángxì*	… (food)	*cài*
detergent	*xǐdíjì*	dislike	*bù xǐhuān*
Deutschmarks	*Déguó mǎkè*	disobey	*bù fúcóng*
develop (film)	*chōngxǐ*	distance	*jùlí*
… (business)	*fāzhǎn*	district	*qū*
dial (v)	*bō*	disturb	*dǎrǎo*
diary	*rìjì*	diversion (road)	*ràodào*
dictionary	*zìdiǎn, cídiǎn*	division	*fēnbù*
die	*sǐ*	divorced	*líhūn le*
diesel	*cháiyóu*	dizzy	*tóuyūn, yūn*
difference	*bùtóng*	do	*gàn, zuò*
different	*bùtóngde*	doctor	*yīshēng, dàifu*
difficult	*nán*	document	*wénjiàn*
difficulty	*kùnnán*	dog	*gǒu*
dilemma	*kùnjìng*	doll	*yángwáwa*
dining car	*cān chē*	dollar (Hong Kong)	*Gǎng bì*
dining room	*cān tīng*	… (US)	*Měi yuàn*
dinner	*wǎncān, zhèngcān*	domestic	*guónèi*
		Don't …	*bié*
diplomat	*wàijiāoguān*	do not have	*méi yǒu*
direct (adj)	*zhíjiē*	door	*mén*
direct dialling	*zhí bō*	double	*shuāng*
direct train	*zhídá chē*	double bed	*shuāngrén chuáng*
direction	*fāngxiàng*		
dirty	*zāng*	double happiness	*shuāngxǐ*
disabled	*cánjí*	double room	*shuāngrén fángjiān*
disagree	*bù tóngyì*		
disappointed	*shīwàng*	downstairs	*lóuxià*

draft	cǎogǎo
drama	xìjù, jù
draw (in sport)	píngjú
… (in gambling)	chōujiǎng
… (v)	chōu
dress (n)	yīfu
dressing	tiáoliào
drink (n)	yǐnliào
… (v)	hē
drive (v)	jià, kāi
driver	sījī
driving licence	jiàshǐ zhízhào
drop (v)	diào
drunk	zuì
dry (adj)	gān
dry clean	gān xǐ
duck	yā
due to	yóuyú
dull (boring)	méi yìsi
… (not sharp)	dùn
dumpling	jiǎozi
during	… de shíhou
dust	huīchén
dustbin	lājī tǒng
dustful	huī
duty (obligation)	zérèn
duty manager	dāngbān jīnglǐ
duty-free	miǎnshuì
dynasty	cháodài, cháo

E

each	měi ge
each other	hùxiāng
ear	ěrduō
early	zǎo
earn	zhuàn, zhèng
earphone	ěrjī
earring	ěrhuán
earth (planet)	dìqiú
… (soil)	tǔdì
earthquake	dìzhèn
east	dōng
easy	róngyi
eat	chī
economical	jīngjìde
economy	jīngjì
economy-class	jīngjì cāng
education	jiàoyù
eel	shànyú
egg (e.g. chicken's)	jī dàn
egg-fried rice	dàn chǎo fàn
eight	bā
either … or …	huòzhě … huòzhě …
elastic	sōngjǐn
election	xuǎnjǔ
electrical	diàn
electrical shop	diànqì shāngdiàn
electricity	diàn

electronic	*diànzǐ*
elementary	*jīchǔ*
eleven	*shíyī*
eloquent	*yǒu kǒucái*
embarrass (v)	*shǐ … fājiǒng*
embarrassing	*fājiǒng, gāngà*
embassy	*shǐguǎn*
emergency (in hospital)	*jízhěn*
emergency exit	*jǐnjí chūkǒu*
emperor	*huángdì*
employee	*gùyuán*
employer	*gùzhǔ*
empress	*nǚhuáng*
empty (adj)	*kōng*
… (v)	*kòngchū, téngchū*
end	*jiéshù*
end of month	*yuè dǐ*
end of year	*nián dǐ*
energetic	*jīnglì chōngpèi*
energy	*jīnglì*
engaged (marriage)	*dìnghūn le*
… (telephone)	*zhànxiàn*
engine	*fādòngjī*
engineer	*gōngchéngshī*
English (language)	*Yīngyǔ, Yīngwén*
enjoy	*xiǎngshòu*
enough	*zúgòu*
enquiries	*wènxùnchù*
enter	*rù nèi*

entertain	*zhāodài, kuǎndài*
enthusiastic	*rèqíng*
entrance	*jìnkǒu, rùkǒu*
envelope	*xìnfēng*
environment	*huánjìng*
equal	*píngděng*
equipment	*shèbèi*
error	*cuòwù*
escalator	*diàntī*
escape	*táopǎo*
especially	*tèbié, géwài*
essential	*jīběnde*
estate agent	*fángdìchǎn dàilǐ*
estimate	*gūjìshù*
… (v)	*gūjì*
Europe	*Ōuzhōu*
eve	*qiánxī*
even (number)	*shuāng*
even if	*jíshǐ*
evening	*wǎnshang*
event	*shìjiàn*
every day	*měi tiān*
every month	*měige yuè*
every week	*měige xīngqī*
everybody	*měige rén*
everything	*yíqiè*
everywhere	*měige dìfang, dàochù*
exact	*zhǔnquè*
exactly	*quèshí*
Exactly (yes)	*Méicuò*

examination	kǎoshì
example: for example	bǐrú
example (model)	bǎngyàng
exceed	chāoguò
excellent	yōuxiù, chūsè
except	chúle
excess luggage	chāozhòng xíngli
exchange	jiāohuàn
exchange rate	duìhuàn lǜ
excited, exciting	jīdòng
excursion	jiāoyóu
excuse	jièkǒu
Excuse me	Duìbùqǐ, Láojià
exercise (one's body)	duànliàn
… (n)	liànxí
exhausted	lèisǐ le
exhibition	zhǎnlǎn
exit	chūkǒu
expect	qīdài
expense	fèiyòng
expensive	guì
experience	jīngyàn, jīnglì
experienced	yǒu jīngyàn
explain, explanation	jiěshì
explosion	bàozhà
export	chūkǒu
express (v)	biǎodá
express train	tèkuài huǒchē

expression (face)	biǎoqíng
… (phrase)	biǎodáfǎ
extension (telephone)	fēnjī
external	wàibù
external use	wài yòng
extinguish (fire)	xīmiè
… (species)	mièjué
extra	duōyú
extra-large	tèdà
eye	yǎnjing
eyebrow	méimao
eyelid	yǎnjiémáo

F

face	liǎn
factory	gōngchǎng
fade (colour)	tuìsè
fair (just)	gōngpíng
… (trade fair)	jiāoyìhuì
fairly	tǐng
faith	xìngyǎng
faithful	zhōngchéng
fake	jiǎde
fall (v)	luò, diào
fall in love	ài shang
false	jiǎde
family	jiātíng
family name	xìng
famous	yǒumíng, zhùmíng

fan	*shànzi*	file	*wénjiàn*
far	*yuǎn*	fill (v)	*tián*
far away	*yuǎn*	… (food)	*xiànr*
fare	*piàojià*	… (tooth)	*bǔyá*
farm	*nóngchǎng*	film (movie)	*diànyǐng*
farm owner	*nóngchǎng zhǔ*	… (for camera)	*jiāojuǎn*
farmer	*nóngmín*	finance	*jīnróng*
fashion	*shízhuāng*	find	*zhǎo*
fast (adj, adv)	*kuài*	fine (adj)	*hǎo*
fast food	*kuài cān*	… (n)	*fákuǎn*
fat (adj)	*pàng*	finger	*shǒuzhǐtou*
fatal	*zhìmìng*	finish (e.g. work)	*xiàbān*
father	*fùqin, bàba*	… (e.g. a project)	*wánchéng*
fault	*cuòwù*		
favourite (adj)	*zuìxǐ'àide*	fire	*huǒ*
fax	*chuánzhēn*	fire brigade	*xiāofáng duì*
fax machine	*chuánzhēn jī*	fire engine	*jiù huǒ chē*
February	*èryuè*	fire extinguisher	*miè huǒ qì*
fed up	*yànfán*	firm (company)	*gōngsī*
fee	*fèi*	… (tough)	*qiángyìng*
feel (v)	*gǎnjué*	first	*dì yī*
female	*nǚde*	first aid	*jí jiù*
feminine	*nǚxìng*	first-class	*tóuděng, shàngděng*
ferment	*fāxiào*		
festival	*jiérì*	first time	*dì yī cì*
fever	*fāshāo*	fish	*yú*
few	*shǎoxǔ, jǐge*	fisherman	*yúmín*
fiancé	*wèihūnfū*	fishing	*diàoyú*
fiancée	*wèihūnqī*	fishing village	*yú cūn*
fight (n)	*dǎzhàng*	fit (healthy)	*jiànkāng*
figure	*shùzì*	… (v)	*héshì*

fitting room	*shìyī shì*	forehead	*qián'é*
five	*wǔ*	foreign	*wàiguóde*
fix (v)	*xiū*	foreign affairs	*wài shì*
flash (for camera)	*shǎnguāngdēng*	foreign office	*wài bàn*
flat (n)	*gōngyù, tàofáng*	foreign guest	*wàibīn*
… (adj)	*píng, biǎn*	foreigner	*wàiguórén*
flat tyre	*méi qì le*	forest	*sēnlín*
flea market	*tiàozao shìchǎng*	forget	*wàngjì*
flee	*táopǎo*	forgive	*yuánliàng*
fleet (navy)	*jiànduì*	fork	*chāzi*
flexible	*línghuó*	form (n)	*biǎogé*
flight	*hángbān, fēijī*	formal, formality	*zhèngshì*
flight number	*hángbān hào*	former	*cóngqiánde, qián*
float (v)	*piāo*		
flood	*hóngshuǐ*	fortnight	*liǎngzhōu*
floor (storey)	*céng*	fortunate	*xìngyùn*
… (ground)	*dìbǎn*	fortune (possession)	*cáichǎn*
flour	*miànfěn*		
flower	*huā*	foster	*fúyǎng*
flu	*liúgǎn, gǎnmào*	foundation	*jīchǔ*
fly	*fēi*	fountain	*quánshuǐ*
fog	*wù*	four	*sì*
food	*fàn*	foyer	*méntīng*
food and vegetable shop	*fùshí diàn*	fracture (broken bones)	*gǔzhé*
food poisoning	*shíwù zhòngdú*	fragile	*xūruò*
foot, feet	*jiǎo*	frankly	*lǎoshí*
football	*zúqiú*	free (have time)	*yǒukòng*
for	*wèi le*	free of charge	*miǎnfèi*
forbid	*bùxǔ, jìnzhǐ*	free, freedom	*zìyóu*
Forbidden City	*Zǐjīn Chéng*	freelance	*zìyóu zhíyè*
		freeze (v)	*dòngjié*

159

freezer	lěngdòngguì
French (language)	Fǎwén
... (people)	Fǎguórén
French franc	Fǎguó fǎláng
frequent (adj)	jīngcháng
fresh	xīnxiān
Friday	xīngqīwǔ
fridge	bīngxiāng
fried noodles	chǎo miàn
friend	péngyou
friendly	yǒuhǎo
friendship	yǒuyì
frightened	hàipà
from	cóng
front	qiánmiàn
frost	shuāng
frozen food	lěngdòng shípǐn
fruit	shuǐguǒ
frustrated	biēqì
fry (v)	jiān
fuel	ránliào
full (e.g. bottle)	mǎn
... (e.g. stomach)	bǎo
function	zuòyòng, gōngnéng
fund	jījīn
fundamental	jīběn
funeral	zànglǐ
funny	huáji
fur	máopí
furniture	jiājù

fussy	luōsuo
future	jiānglái

G

gain (v)	dédào
gallery	huàláng
gallon	jiālún
gambling	dǔbó
game (a form of play)	yóuxì
... (animal)	yěwèi
garage	xiūchēháng
garden	huāyuán
garlic	dàsuàn
gas	méiqì
gate	dàmén
... (at airport)	dēngjīkǒu
general (adj)	zǒngde
... (army)	jiāngjūn
generous	dàfang, kāngkǎi
genius	tiāncái
gentle	wēnróu
gentleman (in 'Ladies and gentlemen')	xiānshēngmen
gentleman	shēnshì
genuine	zhēnde
geography	dìlǐ
get (something)	ná
... (somewhere)	dào
get off (e.g. the bus)	xià (chē)

get on (e.g. the bus)	shàng (chē)	government	zhèngfǔ
		gradual	zhújiàn
get on (with somebody)	xiāngchǔ hěn hǎo	graduate (n)	bìyèshēng
		… (v)	bìyè
ghost	guǐ	gram	kè
gift	lǐwù	grammar	yǔfǎ
ginger	shēngjiāng	grand	hóngwěi
girl	nǚhái	granddaughter	sūnnǚ
girlfriend	nǚpéngyou	grandson	sūnzi
give	gěi	granddad (paternal)	yéye
glass (brittle substance)	bōli	… (maternal)	wàigōng
… (for drinks)	bōlibēi	grandfather (paternal)	zǔfù
glasses	yǎnjìng	… (maternal)	wàizǔfù
gloves	shǒutào	grandma (paternal)	nǎinai
glue	jiāoshuǐ	… (maternal)	wàipó
go	qù	grandmother (paternal)	zǔmǔ
goal (aim)	mùbiāo	… (maternal)	wàizǔmǔ
… (sport)	jìnqiú	grandparents (paternal)	zǔfùmǔ
God	Shàngdì	… (maternal)	wàizǔfùmǔ
golf	gāo'ěrfū	grant (fund)	bǔzhùjīn
good	hǎo	grape	pútao
gold	jīnzi	grapefruit	yòuzi
gold-plated	dù jīn	grass	cǎo
golden	jīnsè	grateful	gǎnjī
good-looking	hǎokàn	grave (n)	fénmù
Good morning	Zǎoshang hǎo	greasy	yóunì
goodbye	zàijiàn	great	wěidà
Goodnight	Wǎn ān		
gorgeous	fēichánghǎo		
gossip (v)	xiánliáo		
govern	guǎnlǐ		

Great Wall	*Chángchéng*	hamburger	*hànbǎobāo*
greedy	*tānlán*	hand	*shǒu*
Greek	*Xīlà*	hand-luggage	*shǒutí xíngli*
green	*lǜsè*	hand-made	*shǒugōng zuòde*
grey	*huīsè*	handbag	*shǒutíbāo*
grill	*kǎo*	handkerchief	*shǒujuàn*
ground	*dì*	handle (n)	*bàr*
ground floor	*yī céng*	… (v)	*duìfu*
group	*xiǎozǔ, tuán*	hang up	*guà qǐlái*
grow	*chéngzhǎng*	happen	*fāshēng*
grow up	*zhǎng dà*	(take place)	
guarantee	*bǎozhèng*	… (coincide)	*gānghǎo*
guest	*kèren*	happy	*gāoxìng*
guesthouse	*bīnguǎn*	harbour (n)	*gǎngwān*
guide: tourist guide	*dǎoyóu*	hard (not soft)	*yìng*
guide (v)	*yǐndǎo*	… (difficult)	*nán*
guidebook	*dǎoyóu shū*	hard-seat	*yìng zuò*
guilty (feeling)	*nèijiù*	hard-sleeper	*yìng wò*
guitar	*jítā*	hard-work	*nǔlì*
gymnasium	*jiànshēnfáng*	hard-working (academic)	*yònggōng*
		hat	*màozi*

H

		hate	*hèn*
habit	*xíguàn*	have	*yǒu*
hair	*máofà*	he	*tā*
… (head hair)	*tóufa*	head	*tóu*
haircut	*jiǎntóufa*	headache	*tóuténg*
hair gel	*fà jiāo*	headphones	*ěrjī*
hairdresser's	*fàláng*	headquarters	*zǒngbù*
hair dryer	*chuīfēngjī*	heal	*quányù*
half (n)	*bàn*	health	*shēntǐ*
ham	*huǒtuǐròu*		

healthy	jiànkāng
hear	tīngdào, tīngshuō
heart	xīnzàng
heart attack	xīnzàngbìng fāzuò
heat rash	fèizi
heat up	rè yīxià
heating	nuǎnqì
heaven	tiāntáng
heavy	zhòng
height (person)	shēngāo
… (object)	gāodù
helicopter	zhíshēng fēijī
hell	dìyù
hello	nǐ hǎo
helmet	tóukuī
help (v)	bāngzhù
Help!	Jiùmìn
hepatitis	gānyán
her ('her mum')	tāde
… ('I saw her')	tā
herb, herbal	cǎoyào
here	zhèr
hers	tāde
hiccup	dǎgé
high	gāo
high school	zhōng xué
hill	shānqiū
him	tā
hire (employ)	gùyòng

… (rent)	zū
his	tāde
history	lìshǐ
hit (v)	dǎ
hobby	àihào
holdings	kònggǔ
holiday	dùjià, jiàqī
home	jiā
homosexual	tóngxìngliàn
honeymoon	mìyuè
Hong Kong	Xiānggǎng
hope	xīwàng
horrible	zāotòu le
horse	mǎ
horse racing	sài mǎ
hospital	yīyuàn
hospitality	hàokè, zhāodài
host	zhǔrén
hostess	nǚzhǔrén
hostility	díyì
hot (chilli)	là
… (food & drinks)	tàng
… (weather)	rè
hot pot	huǒ guō
hot and sour	suān là
hotel	fàndiàn, bīnguǎn, jiǔdiàn
hour	xiǎoshí
house	fángzi
housewife	jiātíng zhǔfù
housework	jiāwùshì

how	*zěnme*	important	*zhòngyào*
How are things?	*zěnme yàng?*	impossible	*bù kěnéng*
How are you?	*zěnme yàng?*	in	*zài*
how far	*duō yuǎn*	include, included	*bāokuò*
how long	*duō jiǔ, duō cháng shíjiān*	indoors	*shìnèi*
		industry	*gōngyè*
how many (small number)	*jǐ*	inexpensive	*bù guì, piányi*
... (large number)	*duō shǎo*	in fact	*shíjì shang*
how old	*duō dà le*	infected	*chuánrǎnde*
How much? (price)	*duō shǎo qián?*	infection	*chuánrǎn, fāyán*
human	*rénlèi*	informal	*bù zhèngshì, suíbiàn*
humid	*cháoshī*		
humour	*yōumò*	information	*xìnxī*
hungry	*è*	information desk	*wènxùn chù*
hundred	*bǎi*	injection	*dǎzhēn, zhùshè*
hurt (v)	*téng*	injure	*shòushāng*
... (emotion)	*shāngxīn*	ink	*mòshuǐ*
husband	*zhàngfu, xiānsheng*	innocent	*wúgū, tiānzhēn*
		insect	*kūnchóng, chóngzi*

I

		inside	*zài ... lǐmiàn*
		insist	*jiānchí*
I	*wǒ*	insomnia	*shīmián*
ice	*bīng*	instant coffee	*sùróng kāfēi*
ice cream	*bīngjilíng*	instead of	*bùshì*
idea	*zhǔyì, xiǎngfǎ*	insult	*wūrǔ*
if	*rúguǒ*	insurance	*bǎoxiǎn*
ill	*bìng le*	intelligent	*cōngmíng*
immediately	*mǎshàng, lìjí*	interest (bank)	*lìxī*
impatient	*bù nàixīn*	... (keen)	*xìngqu*
import	*jìnkǒu*	interesting	*yǒu yìsi*

interested	gǎn xìngqu
international	guójì
interpret, interpreter	fānyì
introduce	jièshào
invite	yāoqǐng, qǐng
invitation	yāoqǐng
Ireland	Ài'ěrlán
Irish	Ài'ěrlánrén
iron	tiě
is	shì
island	dǎo
it	zhège, tā
itchy	yǎng
itinerary	lǚxíng rìchéng
ivory	xiàngyá

J

jacket	shàngyī
jade	yù
jam	guǒjiàng
January	yīyuè
Japan	Rìběn
Japanese (language)	Rìwén
… (people)	Rìběnrén
jasmine tea	mòlìhuā chá
jazz	juéshì yīnyuè
jealous	jídù
jeans	niúzǎikù
jellyfish	hǎizhé

jewellery	shǒushì
Jew	Yóutàirén
job	gōngzuò
jog, jogging	pǎobù
join	cānjiā
joke	xiàohua
journalist	jìzhě
journey	lǚxíng, lǚtú
juice	zhī, shuǐ
July	qīyuè
jump	tiào
jumper	máoyī
June	liùyuè
junk	pòlàn
just (adv)	gāng, cái
… (fair)	gōngpíng

K

keep	liúxià
kettle	shuǐhú
key	yàoshi
kid	xiǎohái
kidney	shènzàng
kill	shā
kilogram	gōngjīn
kilometre	gōnglǐ
kind (n)	zhǒnglèi
… (adj)	hǎoxīn
king	guówáng
kiosk	tíngzi
kiss	wěn, qīnwěn

kitchen	*chúfáng*	last year	*qù nián*
knee	*xīgài*	late	*wǎn*
knickers	*nèikù*	late: be late	*chídào*
knife	*dāo*	lately	*zuìjìn*
knit	*dǎ máoxiàn*	later	*hòulái*
knock	*qiāo*	laugh	*xiào*
knot	*jié*	lavatory	*cèsuǒ*
know about	*zhīdao*	law	*fǎlù*
knowledge	*zhīshi*	lawn	*cǎopíng*
Korea	*Cháoxiǎn*	lawyer	*lùshī*
		laxative	*xièyào*

L

label	*biāoqiān*	lazy	*lǎn*
laces (for shoes)	*xiédài*	lead (electrical)	*diànxiàn*
ladies (toilet)	*nǚ cèsuǒ*	leader	*lǐngdǎo*
… (in 'Ladies and	*nǚshìmen*	leaf	*shùyè*
gentlemen')		leaflet	*chuándān*
lady	*nǚshì*	leak	*lòu*
lager	*píjiǔ*	learn	*xué, xuéxí*
lake	*hú*	leather	*pí*
lamb (meat)	*yángròu*	leave	*líkāi*
… (baby sheep)	*yánggāo*	leave (train)	*fāchē*
lamp	*dēng*	lecturer	*jiǎngshī*
land (v)	*jiàngluò*	left	*zuǒ*
… (n)	*tǔdì*	left-luggage	*xíngli jìcún chù*
lane (on road)	*chēdào*	leg	*tuǐ*
… (street)	*xiàng, hútong*	legal	*héfǎ*
language	*yǔyán*	lemon	*níngméng*
large	*dà*	lend	*jiè*
last month	*shàngge yuè*	lesson	*kè*
last week	*shàngge xīngqī*	let	*ràng*
		letter	*xìn*

letterbox	xìntǒng, xìnxiāng
liberate	jiěfàng
library	túshūguǎn
licence	zhízhào
lid	gàizi
lie (untruth)	shuōhuǎng
lie down	tǎngxià
life ('How is life?')	shēnghuó
… ('Life is precious')	shēngmìng
lifebelt	jiùshēngquān
lift (n)	diàntī
light (not heavy)	qīng
… (n)	dēng
… (e.g. light red)	qiǎn
light bulb	dēng pào
like (v)	xǐhuan
… (similar)	xiàng
likely	kěnéng
limit	xiànzhì
limited company	yǒuxiàn gōngsī
linen (for beds)	chuángdān
… (fabric)	yàmá
linguist	yǔyánxuéjiā
lion	shīzi
lip	zuǐchún
lipstick	kǒuhóng
liquid	yètǐ
liquor	jiǔ
list (n)	mùlù, dānzi

listen	tīng
litter (rubbish)	fèiwù
little	xiǎo
… a little	yìdiǎnr
live	zhù
lobby	qiántíng, dàtīng
lobster	lóngxiā
local	dāngdì
lock	suǒ
lonely	gūdān
long	cháng
… (time only)	jiǔ
long-distance	chángtú
look (v)	kàn
look around	kànkan
look for	zhǎo
loose	sōng
lorry	kǎchē
lose	diūshī
lot, a lot	hěn duō
loud	dàshēngde, chǎo
lounge	kètīng
love	ài
lovely	kě'ài, zhēnhǎo
low	dī
lower (adj)	xià
luck	yùnqi
lucky	yùnqi hǎo
luggage	xíngli
lunch	wǔfàn, zhōngfàn

luxury	*háohuá*
lychee	*lìzhī*

M

machine	*jīqì*
mad	*fēng le*
madam	*nǚshì*
magazine	*zázhì*
magnificent	*hǎojíle*
maid	*nǚ fúwùyuán, nǚ yòngren*
mail	*yóujiàn, xìnjiàn*
mailbox	*xìnxiāng*
main	*zhǔyào*
make	*zuò*
make a reservation	*yùdìng*
make a speech	*jiǎnghuà*
make phonecalls	*dǎ diànhuà*
make-up	*huàzhuāngpǐn*
man, men	*nánde, nánrén*
manager (company)	*jīnglǐ*
... (factory)	*chángzhǎng*
managing director	*zǒng jīnglǐ*
Mandarin	*Pǔtōnghuà, Guóyǔ, Huáyǔ*
manual	*shǒugōng*
manual worker	*gōngrén*
many	*hěnduō*
Mao jacket	*Zhōngshān zhuāng*

map	*dìtú*
March	*sānyuè*
market	*zìyóu shìchǎng*
married	*jiéhūn le*
martial art	*wǔshù*
masses (lots of people)	*qúnzhòng*
masterpiece	*jiézuò*
match (competition)	*bǐsài*
matches	*huǒchái*
material (fabric)	*bùliào*
matter	*shì*
... it doesn't matter	*méi guānxi*
mattress	*diànzi*
may	*kěyǐ, yěxǔ*
May	*wǔyuè*
maybe	*yěxǔ*
me	*wǒ*
meal	*fàn*
mean	*yìsi shì*
meaning	*yìsi*
meat	*ròu*
mechanic	*jìshī, jīxièshī*
medicine	*yào*
medium	*zhōngděng*
medium-sized	*zhōnghào*
meet	*jiànmiàn, jiàndào*
meeting	*huìyì*
meeting place	*jiànmiàn dìdiǎn*
melon	*tiánguā*

member	*chéngyuán*
mend (repair)	*xiū*
men's toilet	*nán cèsuǒ*
menstruate	*lái yuèjīng*
menstruation	*yuèjīng*
mention	*tíqǐ*
menu	*càidān*
... set menu	*tào cài*
message	*kǒuxìn*
metal	*jīnshǔ*
metre	*mǐ*
middle	*zhōngjiān*
middle-class	*zhōngchǎn jiējí*
midnight	*bànyè*
mid-range hotel	*zhōngděng lǚguǎn*
might	*kěnéng, yěxǔ*
mild (taste)	*qīngdàn*
... (weather)	*nuǎnhé*
mile	*yīnglǐ*
military	*jūnshì*
milk	*niúnǎi*
mind: I don't mind	*wǒ bù jièyì*
mine ('It's mine')	*wǒde*
mineral water	*kuàngquán shuǐ*
mini-bus	*xiǎo gōnggòng qìchē, xiǎo miànbāo chē*
minister	*bùzhǎng*
minute ('It's five minutes past one')	*fēn*
... ('I need five minutes')	*fēnzhōng*
minute: just a minute	*děng yīhuǐr*
mirror	*jìngzi*
Miss	*xiǎojiě*
miss (e.g. bus, train)	*wùle, méi gǎnshàng*
... (person)	*xiǎng*
misunderstanding	*wùjiě*
mix (v)	*hùnhé*
modern	*xiàndài*
Monday	*xīngqīyī*
money	*qián*
Mongolian	*Měnggǔ*
Mongolian hot pot	*shuàn yángròu*
month	*yuè*
monthly pass	*yuè piào*
monosodium glutamate	*wèijīng*
moon	*yuèliang*
mooncake	*yuèbǐng*
more	*duō yìdiǎn*
morning	*zǎoshang, shàngwǔ*
mosquito	*wénzi*
mosquito net	*wén zhàng*
mother	*mǔqīn, māma*
motorbike	*mótuōchē*
motorway	*gāosù gōnglù*
mountain	*shān*
moustache	*xiǎohúzi*

mouth	zuǐ, kǒu	necessary	bìyào
movie	diànyǐng	neck	bózi
Mr.	xiānsheng	necklace	xiàngliàn
Mrs.	tàitai, fūren	need	xūyào
mug	gāngzi	needle	zhēn
muscle	jīròu	neighbour	línjū, gébì
menu	càidān	nephew	
mum	māma, niáng	(brother's son)	zhízi
mushroom	mógu	… (sister's son)	wàisheng
music	yīnyuè	nervous	jǐnzhāng
musician	yīnyuèjiā	never	cónglái bù
must	bìxū	new	xīn
mutton	yángròu	news	xīnwén
my	wǒde	newspaper	bàozhǐ
myself	wǒzìjǐ	news-stand	bào tíng
		New Year	xīn nián

N

		… Chinese New Year	Chūnjié
nail (of finger, toe)	zhǐjia	New Zealand	Xīnxīlán
… (metal)	dīngzi	New Zealander	Xīnxīlánrén
… (v)	dìng	next	xià ge
nail clippers	zhǐjia dāo	next day	xià yī tiān, dì èr tiān
naked	luǒtǐ		
name	míngzi	next door	gébì
nap	wǔjiào	next to	pángbiān
napkin (for dining)	cānjīn	next year	míng nián
narrow	zhǎi	nice	hǎo
nationality	guójí	niece (brother's daughter)	zhínǚ
natural	zìrán		
nausea	ěxīn	… (sister's daughter)	wàishēngnǚ
near	jìn		
nearby	fùjìn	night	yèli

night bus	*yèbān chē*
nightclub	*yèzǒnghuì*
nightdress	*shuìyī*
nine	*jiǔ*
no	*bù, bù shì*
nobody	*méirén*
no entry	*jìnzhǐ rù nèi, bù zhǔn rù nèi*
nonsense	*húshuō*
non-smoking	*bù xīyān*
no smoking	*qǐng wù xīyān*
noodles	*miàn, miàntiáo*
noodles in soup	*tāng miàn*
normal	*zhèngcháng*
north	*běi*
northeast	*dōngběi*
northwest	*xīběi*
nose	*bízi*
nosebleeding	*liú bíxuè*
not	*bù, méi*
... (formal)	*wù*
not bad	*bù cuò*
not at all	*nǎli*
note (n)	*tiáozi*
... (v)	*zhùyì*
nothing	*méi shénme*
November	*shíyīyuè*
now	*xiànzài*
number	*hàomǎ, hào*
nurse	*hùshi*
nylon	*nílóng*

O

obvious	*míngxiǎn*
occasionally	*ǒu'ěr*
o'clock	*diǎn, diǎnzhōng*
October	*shíyuè*
odd (strange)	*qíguài*
... (number)	*dān*
offer (price)	*yàojià*
... (v)	*gěi*
offend	*màofàn*
office	*bàngōngshì*
... (branch)	*bànshìchù*
official	*guānfāngde*
often	*chángcháng*
oil	*yóu*
oil painting	*yóu huà*
OK	*hǎode, xíng*
old	*lǎo*
old-fashioned	*lǎoshì, guòshí*
on	*zài ... shàng*
once (one time)	*yícì*
... (formerly)	*céngjīng*
one	*yī*
... (in telephone no. etc.)	*yāo*
onion	*yángcōng*
only	*zhǐyǒu*
open	*kāi*
... (e.g. shops)	*kāimén*
operation (medical)	*kāidāo, shǒushù*

opinion	*yìjiàn*
opportunity	*jīhuì*
opposite	*duìmiàn*
optician	*yǎnjìngdiàn*
optimistic	*lèguān*
or (in statement)	*huòzhě*
... (in question)	*háishi*
orange	*chéngzi, gānzi*
orange juice	*júzi zhī, chéng zhī*
order (in restaurants)	*diǎncài*
... (e.g. in good order)	*zhìxù*
... (in business)	*dìngdān*
ordinary	*pǔtōng*
organisation	*jīgòu; dānwèi*
organise	*zǔzhī*
original (earliest)	*yuánláide*
... (new)	*xīnyǐngde*
other	*biéde*
our, ours	*wǒménde*
outdoors	*lùtiān*
outside	*wàimian*
outskirts	*jiāoqū*
oven	*kǎoxiāng*
over (more than)	*duō*
... (on top)	*zài ... shàng*
overcharge	*duō shōuqián*
overcoat	*dàyī*
overnight	*guòyè*

overweight (person)	*tài pàng le*
owe	*qiàn*
owner	*zhǔrén*
oyster	*mǔlì, háo*
oyster sauce	*háo yóu*

P

pack, packet	*bāo*
page	*yè*
pagoda	*tǎ*
pain, painful	*téng*
painkillers	*zhǐténgyào*
paint (decorator's)	*yóuqī*
... (artist's)	*yóucǎi*
... (painting a house)	*qī*
... (painting a picture)	*huà*
painting	*huà*
pair	*duì*
pal	*huǒbànr*
palace	*gōngdiàn*
Palace Museum	*Gùgōng*
pale	*cāngbái*
pancake	*bǐng*
panda	*xióngmāo*
panic	*fāhuāng*
pants	*kùzi*
paper	*zhǐ*
parcel	*bāoguǒ*

pardon	*duìbùqǐ*	pencil	*qiānbǐ*
parents	*fùmǔ*	penfriend	*bǐyǒu*
park (n)	*gōngyuán*	penicillin	*qīngméisù*
… (v)	*tíng*	pension	*yǎnglǎojīn*
… car park	*tíng chē chǎng*	people	*rén*
… bike park	*cún chē chù*	People's Daily	*Rénmín Rìbào*
partner	*huǒbànr*	P. R. China	*Zhōnghuá Rénmín Gònghéguó*
party (political)	*dǎng*		
… (group)	*tuántǐ*		
… (get-together)	*jùhuì*	pepper	*hújiāo*
pass (v) (move)	*dǐ*	… green pepper (fresh)	*qīng jiāo*
… (in test)	*jígé*		
passenger	*chéngkè, lǚkè*	perfect	*wánměi, wánhǎo*
passport	*hùzhào*	perfume	*xiāngshuǐ*
passport control	*hùzhào jiǎnchá*	perhaps	*yěxǔ*
path	*xiǎolù*	period (of time)	*shíqī*
patient (adj)	*nàixīn*	permission	*jǔnxǔ*
… (n)	*bìngrén*	person	*rén*
pay (v)	*fùqián*	personnel	*rénshì*
… (n)	*gōngzī*	pessimistic	*bēiguān*
peach	*táozi*	petrol	*qìyóu*
pear	*lízi*	petrol station	*jiāyóuzhàn*
pearl	*zhēnzhū*	pharmacy	*yàodiàn*
peanut	*huāshēng*	phone (v)	*dǎ diànhuà*
peas	*wāndòu*	photocopy (v)	*fùyìn*
peasant	*nóngmín*	… (n)	*fùyìnjiàn*
pedestrian crossing	*rénxíng héngdào*	photograph (n)	*zhàopiàn*
		photographer	*shèyǐngshī*
peel (v)	*bō*	phrase book	*xiǎocídiǎn, chángyòngyǔ shǒucè*
… (n)	*pí*		
pen	*bǐ*	piano	*gāngqín*

pick (choose)	tiāo	plenty	hěnduō
pickpocket	xiǎotōu, páshǒu	plum	lǐzi
picnic	yěcān	p.m.	xiàwǔ
picture (film)	diànyǐng	pneumonia	fèiyán
… (painting)	huà	poached egg	hébāo dàn
… (photo)	zhàopiàn	pocket	kǒudài
pig	zhū	point (n)	diǎn
pigeon	gēzi	… (v)	zhǐchū
pill	yàowán	poisonous	yǒudú
pillow	zhěntou	police, policeman	jǐngchá
pillow case	zhěntào	police station	jǐngchá jú, gōng'ān jú
pin	biézhēn		
pineapple	bōluó	polite	yǒu lǐmào
pink	fěnhóngsè	politician	zhèngzhìjiā
pipe	guǎnzi	politics	zhèngzhì
pity: What a pity!	zhēn kěxi!	pond	chítáng
pizza	Yìdàlì xiànrbǐng, písàbǐng	pool (swimming)	yóuyǒng chí
		poor	qióng
place	dìfang	pop music	liúxíng yīnyuè
places of interest	míngshèng gǔjí	popular	shòu huānyíng
plane	fēijī	population	rénkǒu
plant	zhíwù	pork	zhūròu
plasters	chuàngkǒutiē	port	gǎngkǒu
plastic	sùliào	porter	fúwùyuán
plate	pánzi	possible	kěnéng
platform	zhàntái	post (v)	jì
play (v)	wánr	postbox	xìnxiāng
… (n)	huàjù	postcard	míngxìnpiàn
pleasant	yúkuài	post office	yóu jú
please	qǐng	postpone	tuīchí, yánqī
pleased	gāoxìng	potato	tǔdòu

pound (sterling)	*bàng*
pour	*dào*
powder	*fěn*
powdered milk	*nǎi fěn*
power (electricity)	*gōngdiàn*
power cut	*tíng diàn*
prawn	*dàxiā*
precious	*guìzhòng*
prefer	*gèng xǐhuan*
pregnant	*huáiyùn*
prepare	*zhǔnbèi*
prescription (medical)	*yàofāng*
present	*lǐwù*
pretty	*hǎokàn*
price	*jiàgé*
prime minister	*zǒnglǐ, shǒuxiàng*
prince	*wángzǐ*
princess	*gōngzhǔ*
prison	*jiānyù*
private (e.g. private car)	*sīrén*
… (e.g. solve the problem in private)	*sīxià*
prize	*jiǎngpǐn*
problem	*wèntí*
professor	*jiàoshòu*
promise	*bǎozhèng*
pronounce (read)	*niàn*
prostitute	*jìnǚ*
protect	*bǎohù*

proud	*jiāo'ào*
public	*gōnggòng*
public phone	*gōngyòng diànhuà*
public relation	*gōng guān*
pull (v)	*lā*
pullover	*tàotóu máoyī*
pump (for bike)	*dǎqìtǒng*
pure	*chún*
purple	*zǐsè*
purse	*qiánbāo*
put	*fàng*
push (v)	*tuī*
pyjamas	*shuìyī*

Q

quality	*zhìliàng*
quarter: a quarter (fraction)	*sì fēn zhī yī*
quarter of an hour	*yí kè*
queen (the ruling monarch)	*nǚwáng*
… (wife of the king)	*wánghòu*
question (n)	*wèntí*
… (v)	*tíwèn*
queue (v)	*páiduì*
… (n)	*duì*
quick, quickly	*kuài*
quiet	*ānjìng*
quite	*xiāngdāng, bǐjiào*

R

rabbit	tùzi
race (sport)	bǐsài
racket	qiúpāi
radiator	nuǎnqìpiàn
radio	shōuyīnjī
rail: by rail	zuò huǒchē
railway	tiělù
rail ticket	huǒchē piào
railway station	huǒchē zhàn
rain (v)	xiàyǔ
… (n)	yǔ
raincoat	yǔyī
rare	xīyǒu
rash	pízhěn
rat	lǎoshǔ
rate (exchange rate)	duìhuànlǜ
raw (meat)	shēng
… (material)	yuán
razor	tìhúdāo, tìxūdāo
reach	gòu
read (book, newspaper)	kàn
read aloud	dú, niàn
ready	zhǔnbèi hǎo le
real, really	zhēn de
rear	hòumian
reason	yuányīn
reasonable (price)	hélǐ
… (person)	jiǎnglǐde

receipt	shōujù, fāpiào
recently	zuìjìn
reception (in hotel)	fúwùtái
… (welcome party)	zhāodàihuì
receptionist	fúwùyuán
recipe	càipǔ
recognise (somebody)	rènchū
… (characters)	rènshí
recommend	tuījiàn
record (music)	chàngpiàn
… (written document)	jìlù
recorded delivery	guàhào
red	hóngsè
red wine	hóng pútaojiǔ
refrigerator	bīngxiāng
refund	tuìkuǎn
registered	guàhào
relative (family)	qīnqi
relaxing	fàngsōng, shūfu
reliable	kěkào
religion	zōngjiào
remains (of old city)	yízhǐ
remember	jìde
remote	piānpì
rent (v)	zū
… (n)	fángzū
rent: for rent	chūzū
repair	xiū

repeat	*chóngfù, zài shuō yībiàn*	ring (on finger)	*jièzhi*
representative	*dàibiǎo*	ring road	*huánchéng lù*
request	*qǐngqiú*	ripe (fruit)	*shú*
rescue (v)	*jiù*	rip-off	*qiāo zhúgàng*
reservation, reserve	*yùdìng*	risk, risky	*wēixiǎn*
		river	*hé*
rest	*xiūxi*	road	*lù*
rest-room	*xiūxishì*	roadsign	*lùbiāo*
restaurant	*cānguǎn, fànguǎn*	roadworks	*xiūlù*
		roast	*kǎo*
restaurant car	*cān chē*	rob	*qiǎng*
retired	*tuìxiū le*	rock	*shítou*
return (v) (e.g. book)	*huán*	romance	*làngmàn*
		Rome	*Luómǎ*
… (e.g. home)	*huí*	roof	*fángdǐng*
return ticket	*láihuí piào*	room	*fángjiān*
reverse charge call	*duìfāng fùkuǎn*	room service	*fángjiān fúwù*
rheumatism	*fēngshībìng*	rope	*shéngzi*
rice (uncooked rice)	*dàmǐ*	rose	*méiguì*
		roughly	*dàyuē*
… (cooked rice)	*mǐfàn*	round (adj)	*yuán*
rice wine	*mǐ jiǔ*	route	*lùxiàn*
rich (person)	*fù, yǒuqián*	rubber (material)	*xiàngjiāo*
… (resources)	*fēngfù*	… (eraser)	*xiàngpí*
ride (bycicle, horse)	*qí*	rubbish (waste)	*lājī*
		rude	*méi lǐmào, cūlǔ*
ridiculous	*huāngtang, kěxiào*	rug	*xiǎo dìtǎn*
		ruins	*fèixū*
right (not left)	*yòu*	run	*pǎo*
… (correct)	*duì*	Russia	*Éguó*
right-handed	*zuǒ piězi*		

S

sad	*nánguò*
safe	*ān'quán*
safety pin	*biézhēn*
sailor	*shuǐshǒu*
salad	*shālà*
salary	*gōngzī*
sales	*xiāoshòu, tuīxiāo*
salesperson	*tuīxiāoyuán*
salmon	*dà mǎhāyú*
salt	*yán*
salty	*xián*
same	*yíyàng*
sand	*shāzi*
sandals	*liángxié*
sandwich	*sānmíngzhì*
sanitary towel	*wèishēng jīn*
satisfactory	*lìngrén mǎnyìde*
Saturday	*xīngqīliù*
sauce	*zhī, jiàng*
saucepan	*guō*
saucer	*diézi*
sauna	*zhēngqìyù*
sausage	*xiāngcháng*
sautéed	*yóumèn*
save (life)	*jiù*
... (money, time)	*jiéyuē*
say	*shuō*
scarf	*wéijīn*
scenery	*fēngjǐng*
scent (of perfume)	*xiāngwèi*
schedule	*rìchéng*
school	*xuéxiào*
... primary school	*xiǎoxué*
... secondary school	*zhōngxué*
... university	*dàxué*
science	*kēxué*
scissors	*jiǎndāo*
Scotland	*Sūgélán*
Scottish	*Sūgélánrén*
scrambled egg	*chǎo jīdàn*
scratch (v)	*zhuāyixià, huáyixià*
screw (n)	*luósīdīng*
screwdriver	*luósīdāo*
sea	*hǎi*
seafood	*hǎixiān*
seal (for name)	*túzhāng*
search	*zhǎo*
seasick	*yùnchuán*
season	*jìjié*
seat	*zuòwèi*
seat belt	*ānquándài*
seaweed (edible)	*hǎicǎo, zǐcài*
second (adj)	*dì'èr*
... (of time)	*miǎo*
... just a second	*děng yīxià, děng yīhuǐr*
second-class	*èr děng*

second-hand (e.g. shop)	jiùhuò
secret	mìmì
secretary	mìshū
security check	ānquán jiǎnchá
see	kànjiàn
See you later	huíjiàn
seem	sìhū
seldom	hěnshǎo
self	zìjǐ
self-introduction	zìwǒ jièshào
self-service	zìzhù
sell	mài
send (mail)	jì
… (person)	pài
senior (e.g. engineer)	gāojí
sense	gǎnjué
… it doesn't make sense	… méi dàoli
sensible (idea)	yǒu dàolǐ
… (person)	jiǎng dàolǐ
sensitive	mǐngǎn
sentence (n)	jùzi
separate	fēnkāi
September	jiǔyuè
serious	yánzhòng
service	fúwù
service charge	xiǎo fèi
serviette	cānjīn
sesame	zhīma
sesame oil	xiāng yóu

set off	chūfā
settle down	ān'dùn xiàlai
seven	qī
several	jǐge
sew	féng
sewing machine	féngrèn jī
sex	xìng
sexy	xìnggǎn
shadow	yǐngzi
shake (v)	yáo
shake hands	wò shǒu
shall	jiāng, yào
shallow (water)	qiǎn
shame: What a shame!	zhēn kěxī
shampoo	xǐfàyè
share	héyòng
sharp (knife)	kuài
… (pain)	lìhai
shave	guā
shaver	tìxūdāo
she	tā
sheep	yáng
sheet (for beds)	chuángdān
shelf	jiàzi
shell	kér
sherry	xuělìjiǔ
ship	chuán
shirt	chènyī
shivery	fādǒu
shock	chījīng

shoe	*xiézi*	signal	*xìnhào*
shoe polish	*xié yóu*	signpost	*lùbiāo*
shoe and hat shop	*xiémào diàn*	sightseeing	*guānguāng*
shop (n)	*shāngdiàn*	silence, silent	*chénmò*
shop assistant	*shòuhuòyuán*	silk	*sīchóu*
shopping	*mǎi dōngxi*	silly	*bèn, chǔn*
shop window	*chú chuāng*	silver	*yín*
short (thing, time)	*duǎn*	simple	*jiǎndān*
… (person)	*ǎi*	sin	*zuìguo*
shorts	*duǎnkù*	since	*zìcóng*
should	*yīnggāi*	sing	*chànggē*
shoulder	*jiānbǎng*	Singapore	*Xīnjiāpō*
shout	*hǎn*	single (room)	*dānrén*
show (v)	*xiǎnshì, chūshì*	… (person)	*dānshēn*
shower (wash)	*línyù*	… (ticket)	*dānchéng*
… (rain)	*zhènyǔ*	sink	*shuǐchí*
shower cap	*línyùmào*	sir	*xiānsheng*
show-off	*chūfēngtou*	sister (elder)	*jiějie*
shrimps	*xiā*	… (younger)	*mèimei*
shrink (clothes)	*suōshuǐ*	sisters	*jiěmèi*
shut	*guān*	sit, sit down	*zuò*
Shut up!	*Zhù zuǐ*	sitting room	*kè tīng*
shy	*hàixiū*	situation	*qíngkuàng, xíngshì*
Sichuan cuisine	*Chuān cài*		
Sichuan pepper	*huājiāo*	six	*liù*
sick	*shēngbìng*	size	*hàomǎ, chǐcùn*
side	*biān*	ski (v)	*huáxuě*
sidewalk	*rénxíngdào*	skin	*pífū*
sign (n)	*biāozhì*	skirt	*qúnzi*
… (v)	*qiān, qiānmíng, qiānzì*	sky	*tiān*
		sleep	*shuìjiào*

sleeping pill	ānmiányào	socket	chāzuò
sleepy	kùn	soda	sūdǎ
sleeve	xiùzi	sofa	shāfā
slide (photo)	huàndēngpiàn	soft	ruǎn
slide projector	huàndēng jī	soft drinks	ruǎn yǐnliào
slim	miáotiao	soft-sleeper	ruǎn wò
slippery	huá	sold out	mài guāng le
slow, slowly	màn	soldier	shìbīng
small	xiǎo	sole (of shoes)	xiédǐ
small inn	lǚshè	solid (not liquid)	gùtǐ
smallpox	tiānhuā	… (strong)	jiēshi
smart	shuài	some	yìxiē
smashing	bàngjíle	somebody	yǒurén
smell (v)	wén	sometimes	yǒu shíhou
… (n)	wèidao	somewhere	mǒudì
smile	wēixiào	son	érzi
smoke (v)	xīyān, chōuyān	song	gē
smooth	shùnlì	son-in-law	nǚxu
snack bar	kuàicān diàn	soon	mǎshàng
snake	shé	sore	téng
snob	shìlìyǎn	sore throat	sǎngzi téng, houlóng téng
snow (v)	xiàxuě		
… (n)	xuě	sorry	duìbùqǐ
so (as a result)	suǒyǐ	sound (n)	shēngyīn
… (extremely)	zhème	sound: it sounds	tīng qǐlái
soaked	shītòule	soup	tāng
soap	xiāngzào, féizào	sour	suān
soccer	zúqiú	south	nán
socialism	shèhuìzhǔyì	southeast	dōngnán
society	shèhuì	southwest	xī'nán
socks	wàzi	souvenir	jìniànpǐn

soy sauce	*jiàngyóu*	spring onion	*cōng*
space	*kōngjiān*	spring rolls	*chūnjuǎn*
spade	*tiěqiāo*	square	*guǎngchǎng*
Spain	*Xībānyá*	(open space)	
spare	*duōyúde*	… (shape)	*fāng*
speak	*shuō, jiǎng*	… (shape)	*fāng*
special	*tèbié*	squash	*bìqiú*
specialist	*zhuānjiā*	stairs	*lóutī*
speciality	*tècháng*	stall	*tān, tíng*
… (food)	*fēngwèi*	stamps	*yóupiào*
spectacles	*yǎnjìng*	stand (v)	*zhànzhe*
speed	*sùdù*	stand: I can't	*wǒ shòu bù liǎo*
speed limit	*sùdù xiànzhì*	stand …	
spell (v)	*pīn*	standard	*biāozhǔn*
spend (money, time)	*huā*	stapler	*dìngshūjī*
		star (in the sky)	*xīngxing*
… (festival)	*guò*	… (celebrity)	*míngxīng*
spicy	*là*	stare	*dīngzhe*
spider	*zhīzhū*	start	*kāishǐ*
spirit (drink)	*báijiǔ*	starter (meal)	*tóupán*
spoil	*huǐle*	starving	*èsǐle*
sponge	*hǎimián*	state (in USA)	*zhōu*
spoon	*sháozi*	station	*zhàn*
sport	*yùndòng*	statue	*sùxiàng*
spot	*diǎn*	stay	*dāi*
… (on face)	*fēncì*	steak	*niúpái*
spouse	*ài'rén, pèi'ǒu*	steal	*tōu*
spray (v)	*sǎ*	steamed buns	*mántou*
spring (season)	*chūntiān*	steamed buns with fillings	*bāozi*
… (water)	*quán*	steep	*dǒu*
Spring Festival	*Chūn Jié*	steering wheel	*fāngxiàng pán*
		step (n)	*bùzi*

... (stairs)	*táijiē*	strong (person)	*zhuàng*
stereo	*lìtǐshēng*	... (thing)	*jiēshi*
sterling (£)	*Yīng bàng*	... (taste)	*nóng*
stew	*dùn, shāo*	stuck	*qiǎzhùle*
sticky	*zhān, nián*	student	*xuésheng*
stiff	*yìngbāngbāng*	study	*xuéxí, xué*
still (adv)	*réngrán*	stupid	*bèn*
sting (v)	*zhē, dīng*	style (clothing)	*shìyàng*
stir-fry	*chǎo*	suburb	*jiāoqū*
stock (goods)	*kùcún, cúnhuò*	succeed	*chénggōng*
stock exchange	*gǔpiào shìchǎng*	suddenly	*tūrán*
stomach	*wèi, dùzi*	sugar	*táng*
stomach-ache	*wèiténg, dùzi téng*	suggestion	*jiànyì*
stone	*shítou*	suit (clothing)	*tàozhuāng*
stop	*tíng*	... (v)	*shìhé*
store	*shāngdiàn*	suitable	*héshì*
storm	*bàofēngyǔ*	suitcase	*shǒutíxiāng, xiāngzi*
storey	*céng*	summer	*xiàtiān*
story	*gùshi*	sun	*tàiyang*
straight	*zhí*	Sunday	*xīngqītiān, xīngqīrì*
straight ahead	*yìzhí zǒu*		
strange	*qíguài*	sunglasses	*tàiyangjìng*
stranger	*shēngrén*	sunny	*qíngtiān*
strawberry	*cǎoméi*	sunrise	*rìchū*
stream	*xiǎoxī*	suntan lotion	*fángshài yóu*
street	*jiē*	super	*chāo*
strike: on strike	*bàgōng*	superb	*hǎojíle, fēicháng hǎo*
string	*shéngzi*		
stroke	*zhòngfēng*	supermarket	*chāojí shìchǎng*
stroll	*sànbù*	supper	*wǎnfàn*
		support	*zhīchí*

sure	quèxìng	take photograph	zhàoxiàng
surname	xìng	talk	shuōhuà
surprised	chījīng	tall	gāo
swallow (v)	yàn, tūn	tank	tǎnkè
… (n)	yànzi	tangerine	júzi
sweat (v)	chūhàn	Taoism	Dàojiào
… (n)	hàn	tape	cídài
sweet and sour	táng cù	tape recorder	lùyīn jī
sweater	máoyī	taste (n)	wèidao
Sweden	Ruìdiǎn	… (v)	cháng
sweet (adj)	tián	taxi	chūzūchē
… (n)	táng	tea	chá
swell (v)	zhǒng	tea house	chá guǎn
swim	yóuyǒng	teach	jiāo
swimming pool	yóuyǒng chí	teacher	lǎoshī
swimsuit	yóuyǒngyī	teacup	chábēi
switch on	kāi	teapot	cháhú
switch off	guān	teenager	qīngshàonián
swollen	zhǒngle	telegram	diànbào
sympathy	tóngqíng	telephone (n)	diànhuà
symptom	zhèngzhuàng	… (v)	dǎ diànhuà
synthetic	rénzàode	telephone booth	diànhuà tíng
		telephonist	diànhuà jiēxiànyuán

T

		television	diànshì
table	zhuōzi	tell	gàosu
tablet (drug)	yàopiàn	temperature (weather)	qìwēn
tailor's	cáifeng diàn		
take	ná	… (fever)	fāshāo
take care	duō bǎozhòng	… take one's temperature	liáng tǐwēn
take off (e.g. plane)	qǐ fēi		
… (e.g. clothes)	tuō	temple	miào

Temple of Heaven	*Tiāntán*
temporary	*línshí*
ten	*shí*
ten thousand	*yī wàn*
tenant	*fángkè*
tennis	*wǎngqiú*
tennis court	*wǎngqiú chǎng*
tent	*zhàngpeng*
term (at university)	*xuéqī*
terrible	*zāotòule*
terrific	*bàngjíle*
Thailand	*Tàiguó*
thanks, thank you	*xièxie*
that	*nà*
theatre	*jùyuàn*
their, theirs	*tāménde*
then	*ránhòu*
there	*nàr*
thermometer	*wēndùjì, tǐwēnbiǎo*
thermos flask	*rèshuǐpíng*
these	*zhèxiē, zhèixiē*
they, them	*tāmen*
thick	*hòu*
thief	*xiǎotōu*
thigh	*dàtuǐ*
thin (e.g. sheet)	*báo*
... (e.g. rope)	*xì*
... (not fat)	*shòu*
thing	*dōngxi*
think	*xiǎng*
thirsty	*kě*
this	*zhè, zhèi*
this afternoon	*jīntiān xiàwǔ*
this month	*zhège yuè*
this morning	*jīntiān zǎoshang*
this week	*zhège xīngqī*
this year	*jīn nián*
those	*nàxiē, nèixiē*
thousand	*qiān*
thread	*xiàn*
three	*sān*
throat	*sǎngzi, hóulóng*
throat lozenges	*qīnghóu yào*
through	*jīngguò*
throw	*rēngdiào*
thumb	*mǔzhǐ*
thunder	*léi*
Thursday	*xīngqīsì*
Tibet	*Xīzàng*
ticket	*piào*
ticket office	*shòupiào chù*
ticket office for foreigners	*wàibīn shòupiào chù*
tie	*lǐngdài*
tight	*jǐn*
tights	*liánkùwà*
time	*shíjiān*
... What time is it?	*jǐ diǎn le?*
timetable	*shíkèbiǎo*
tin	*guàntou*
tin-opener	*kāi guàntoudāo*

tiny (size)	*hěnxiǎo*	touch (v)	*chùmō*
… (quantity)	*hěnshǎo*	touched (moved)	*gǎndòng*
tip	*xiǎofèi*	tough (meat)	*lǎo*
tire	*lúntāi*	… (difficult)	*bù róngyi*
tired	*lèi*	tour (n)	*lǚyóu*
toast (bread)	*kǎomiànbāo*	tourist	*yóukè*
… (v)	*zhùjiǔ*	tourist coach	*lǚyóu chē*
tobacco	*yāncǎo*	tourist guide	*dǎoyóu*
today	*jīntiān*	towel	*máojīn*
toe	*jiǎozhǐtou*	town	*chéngshì*
tofu	*dòufu*	town centre	*shì zhōngxīn*
together	*yìqǐ*	toy	*wánjù*
toilet	*cèsuǒ*	tradition, traditional	*chuántǒng*
toilet paper	*wèishēng zhǐ*		
tomato	*xīhóngshì*	traffic	*jiāotōng*
tomorrow	*míngtiān*	traffic jam	*jiāotōng dǔsè*
tongue	*shétou*	traffic light	*hónglǜdēng*
tonight	*jīntiān wǎnshang, jīnwǎn*	traffic policeman	*jiāotōng jǐng*
		train	*huǒchē*
tonsils	*biǎntáoxiàn*	train: by train	*zuò huǒchē*
too (extremely)	*tài*	train station	*huǒchē zhàn*
… (also)	*yě*	train ticket	*huǒchē piào*
tooth	*yá*	tram	*diànchē*
toothache	*yáténg*	trainers	*yùndòngxié*
toothbrush	*yáshuā*	translate, translator	*fānyì*
toothpaste	*yágāo*	travel	*lǚyóu*
top (on top of)	*zài … shàngtou*	travel agent	*lǚxíngshè*
… (n)	*dǐng*	traveller's cheque	*lǚxíng zhīpiào*
torch	*diàntǒng*	tray	*chápán*
total	*zǒngshù*	treatment (medical)	*zhìliáo*

tree	*shù*
tremendous	*hǎojíle, liǎobùqǐ*
trendy	*shímáo*
tricky	*nánbàn*
trim (haircut)	*xiūxiu*
trip	*lǚtú, yìlù*
tropical	*rèdài*
trouble	*máfan*
trousers	*kùzi*
truck	*kǎchē*
true	*zhēnde*
truth	*shíhuà, shìshí*
try	*shìshi*
T-shirt	*tìxùshān*
tube (rail)	*dìtiě*
Tuesday	*xīngqī'èr*
tuition (school fee)	*xuéfèi*
… (academic help)	*fúdǎo*
tunnel	*suìdào*
turkey	*huǒjī*
turn (v)	*guǎiwān*
… It's my turn	*lún dào wǒ le*
turning (in road)	*zhuǎnwān*
TV	*diànshì*
twice	*liǎngcì*
twin beds	*liǎngge dānrénchuáng*
twins	*shuāngbāotāi*
two	*èr*
… (in telling the time, etc.)	*liǎng*

type (v)	*dǎzì*
typewriter	*dǎzìjī*
typhoid	*shānghán*
typical	*diǎnxíng*
typist	*dǎzìyuán*
tyre	*lúntāi*

U

ugly	*nánkàn*
umbrella	*yǔsǎn*
uncle (father's elder brother)	*bófù*
… (father's younger brother)	*shūshu*
… (mother's brothers)	*jiùjiu*
… (father's sister's husband)	*gūfù*
… (mother's sister's husband)	*yífù*
uncomfortable	*bù shūfu*
under	*zài … dǐxia*
underdone (meat)	*bùshú*
underground (rail)	*dìtiě*
underground pass	*dìxià tōngdào*
underpants	*nèikù*
understand	*dǒng*
understanding	*lǐjiě*
under-salted	*dàn*
underwear	*nèiyī*
uneatable	*bù néngchī*
undress	*tuō yīfu*

unemployed	*shīyè*	valid (e.g. ticket)	*yǒuxiào*
unfair	*bù gōngpíng*	valley	*shāngǔ*
United States	*Měiguó*	valuables	*guìzhòngwù*
university	*dàxué*	value (n)	*jiàzhí*
unless	*chúfēi*	van	*xiǎo yùnhuòchē*
unlock	*kāi*	variety	*gèzhǒnggèyàng*
unwell	*bù hǎo*	vary	*bù yíyàng*
until	*zhídào*	vase	*huāpíng*
unusual	*bù chángjiàn*	vegetables	*shūcài*
up, upper	*shàng*	vegetarian	*chī sù*
upper-class	*shàngcéng shèhuì, shàngděng jiēcéng*	vegetarian food	*sù cài, sù shí*
		very	*hěn*
upmarket	*gāodàng*	very much	*tài … le, hěn, shífēn*
upset	*bù'ān*		
upset stomach	*wèi bù shūfu*	vest	*bèixīn*
upstairs	*lóushàng*	video	*lùxiàng*
urgent	*jí*	video camera	*shèxiàng jī*
urine	*niào, xiǎobiàn*	video cassette	*lùxiàng dài*
us	*wǒmen*	video recorder	*lùxiàng jī*
use	*yòng*	view (n)	*jǐng*
used	*yòngguòde*	village	*cūnzi*
useful	*yǒuyòng*	vinegar	*cù*
usual, usually	*píngcháng*	vineyard	*pútaoyuán*
		visa	*qiānzhèng*

V

vacancy (at hotels)	*kòng fángjiān*	visability	*néngjiàndù*
… (job)	*kòngquē*	visit (e.g. museums)	*cānguān*
vacation	*jiàqī*	vitamin	*wéishēngsù*
vacuum cleaner	*xīchén qì*	voice	*shēngyīn*
		vomit	*tù*

waist	*yāo*
waistcoat	*xīfú bèixīn*
wait	*děng*
waiter, waitress	*fúwùyuán, zhāodài*
waiting-room (train station)	*hòuchē shì*
… (in hospitals)	*hòuzhěn shì*
wake up	*xǐng lái*
Wales	*Wēi'ěrshì*
walk	*zǒulù*
walking stick	*guǎi gùn*
walkman	*xiùzhēn fàngyīnjī*
wallet	*qiánbāo*
want	*xiǎng*
war	*zhànzhēng*
ward (in hospital)	*bìngfáng*
warm (weather)	*nuānhé*
… (person)	*hǎoxīn*
warn, warning	*jǐnggào*
was	*shì*
wash	*xǐ*
wash basin	*xǐshǒu chí*
washing machine	*xǐyī jī*
washing powder	*xǐyī fěn*
washing-up	*xǐwǎn*
wasp	*huángfēng*
waste (v)	*làngfèi*
… (n)	*lājī*

watch (wrist-watch)	*shǒubiǎo*
… (v)	*kàn*
water	*shuǐ*
watercolour	*shuǐcǎihuà*
waterfall	*pùbù*
waterproof	*fángshuǐ*
wave (sea)	*hǎilàng*
wax	*là*
way: this way, please	*qǐng zhè biān zǒu*
way (route)	*lù*
… (method)	*bànfǎ*
way out	*chūkǒu*
we	*wǒmen*
weak (person)	*ruò*
… (drink)	*dàn*
wealthy	*fù*
wear	*chuān*
weather	*tiānqì*
weather forecast	*tiānqì yùbào*
wedding	*hūnlǐ*
Wednesday	*xīngqīsān*
week	*xīngqī, zhōu*
weekend	*zhōumò*
weight	*zhòngliàng*
weight limit	*zhòngliàng xiànzhì*
weird	*guài*
welcome	*huānyíng*
well (adv)	*hǎo*
… (n)	*shuǐjǐng*

well-done (meal)	lǎoyìdiǎn	wig	jiǎfà
were	shì	will (future tense)	jiāng, yào
west	xī	… (determined)	yídìng
Western food	Xī cān	willing	yuànyi
Western-style	xīshì	win	yíng
wet	shī	wind	fēng
what	shénme	window	chuānghu
What date…?	jǐ hào	windscreen	dǎngfēng bōli
What day…?	xīngqī jǐ	windy	guāfēngle, qǐfēngle
What time…?	jǐ diǎn		
wheel	lúnzi	wine	pútaojiǔ
wheelchair	lúnyǐ	wine glass	jiǔ bēi
when	shénme shíhou	wing	chìbǎng
where	nǎr, shénme dìfang	winter	dōngtiān
		winter holiday (for school)	hánjià
whereabouts	nǎlǐ		
which	nǎ, něi	wire	tiěsī
while	zài … de shíhou	wireless	wúxiàndiàn
… for a while	yīhuǐr	wish	xīwàng
whisky	wēishìjì	with	hé, gēn
whisper (v)	xiǎoshēng de shuō	without	méiyǒu
		witness	zhèngrén
white	báise	witty	huìxié
white wine	bái pútaojiǔ	woman, women	nǚde, nǚrén
who	shéi, shuí	Women's toilet	nǚ cèsuǒ
whole	zhěnggè	wonderful	hǎojíle, tàihǎole
whose	shéide, shuíde	wonton soup	húntun tāng
why	wèishénme	wood	mùtou
wide	kuān	woods	shùlín
widow	guǎfu	wool	yángmáo
wife	qīzi, tàitai, fūren	word	cí

work	gōngzuò
working-class	gōngrén jiējí
work: it doesn't work	huài le
world	shìjiè
worm	chóngzi
worry, worried	zhāojí
worse than	bǐ … gèng huài
worst	zuìhuài
would like	xiǎng
wounded (injured)	shòushāng le
wrap up	bāo qǐlai
wrist	shǒuwàn
write	xiě
writer	zuòjiā
writing paper	xiězì zhǐ
wrong	cuò
wrong: What's wrong?	zěnme le?

| X-ray | āikèsī guāng |

yacht	yóutǐng
Yangtze River	Cháng Jiāng
year	nián
yellow	huáng
Yellow River	Huáng Hé
yes	shì de, shì
yesterday	zuótiān

yet: not yet	hái méiyǒu
yoghurt	suānnǎi
you (singular)	nǐ
… (plural)	nǐmen
young	niánqīng
your, yours (singular)	nǐde
… (plural)	nǐménde
youth	qīngchūn, qīngnián
yuan (Chinese currency)	yuán

zero	líng
zip	lāliàn
zoo	dòngwuyuán
zoom lens	biàn jiāo jìngtóu

BBC Books publishes a range of products in the following languages:

ARABIC	GREEK	POLISH
CHINESE	HINDI URDU	RUSSIAN
CZECH	ITALIAN	SPANISH
FRENCH	JAPANESE	THAI
GERMAN	PORTUGUESE	TURKISH

For a catalogue please contact:
BBC Books,   Tel: 01624 675137
Book Service by Post,   Fax: 01624 670923
PO Box 29,
Douglas,
Isle of Man,
IM99 1BQ

BBC books are available at all good bookshops or direct from the
publishers as above.

Developed by BBC Languages
Project Management: Stenton Associates
Design: Steve Pitcher

Published by BBC Books
A division of BBC Worldwide Ltd
Woodlands, 80 Wood Lane, London W12 0TT

ISBN 0 563 40044 7

First published 1996

Text and cover printed in Great Britain by
Clays Ltd, St Ives Plc